LOST AND FOUND

A Hidden Child of the Holocaust
Comes out of Hiding

by Chaya Bressler Subar

Copyright © 2024
by Chaya Bressler Subar

All rights reserved
No part of this publication may be translated, reproduced, stored in a retrieval system or transmitted in any form or by any means, electronic, mechanical, photocopying, recording or otherwise, without permission in writing from the publishers.

LIFESTORIES UNLIMITED PUBLISHING

in conjunction with
IP Integral Publishers

4 Katznelbogen, Jerusalem, Israel
Telephone: 052 763 9137
strombergec@gmail.com

Graphics by Feige Savitsky
Cover Design by Rachel Coten

Paperback: ISBN: 979-8-9931673-0-5
Ebook: ISBN: 979-8-9931673-1-2

First Edition July 2024
Second Edition February 2025

Table of Contents

Acknowledgements V

Foreword VII

Preface IX

Prologue XIII

Chapter 1   Into the Night 1

Chapter 2   Wanja's Trees 7

Chapter 3   "Lady, don't you want to live?" 17

Chapter 4   In the Belly of the Beast 24

Chapter 5   After the War 31

Chapter 6   Ansbach 46

Chapter 7   The Long Road Out 53

Chapter 8   America! 66

Chapter 9   A Working Girl 78

Chapter 10   Returning Home 94

Chapter 11   Bay 5 on Brighton Beach 135

Chapter 12   Joy and Happiness - and then Reality 141

Chapter 13   Aliya 169

Chapter 14   The Trip to Poland 181

Family Pictures 201

ACKNOWLEDGEMENTS

My initial goal was to write my life's story to share with my immediate family. But one of my grandchildren convinced me to have my story written for a wider audience.

"There is so much to learn from you," they would always say. So here I am with my story.

Who do I thank for giving me this opportunity? First and foremost, I thank my Best Friend. He has taught me all that I know. Do you realize that we probably share the same Best Friend – G-O-D.

I thank my mother for giving me life and my father for saving my life.

I thank my adopted parents in Poland for giving me unconditional love which has stayed with me and nurtured me throughout my life.

I thank Yossi Yeinan, my eldest son, who immersed himself in genealogy and did extensive research about my family. I always thought I was all alone, but his research showed me that I had hundreds of souls as part of my family. Due to the Shoah, I never met them, but I was not alone.

I thank the joint efforts of Dr. Eliya and Mrs. Esther Chana Stromberg, professional writers, who brought this book to life. Thank you beyond words!

I thank countless folks who passed through my life and taught me what goodness and sharing is and much, much more. I also met folks who were filled with so much bitterness and anger, they taught me how NOT to be.

And I thank my grandchildren who helped me keep my promise to my Best Friend that I would give Him back Jews. And to this day, they give me great joy and pride in the kind of human beings they are.

FOREWORD

Almost four thousand years ago, our forefather Avraham was born. He came on to the stage during an era of paganism, and lived in a world devoid of knowledge of the Creator. He was raised by idolators, and lived amongst people to whom the concept of monotheism was anathema, and to whom the idea of a divine morality was foreign.

In such a world, Avraham came to know the Creator on his own, when he was all of three years of age. He realized that G-d exists, that the Almighty must have created the world for a reason, and that one can turn to Him for aid, and for a relationship. Lastly, he realized that the aforesaid relationship must perforce consist of continually choosing to follow in G-d's ways.

The book you are holding is the story of a woman who lived many millennia after Avraham, but in her own way, had a similar experience. Klara Bressler Subar (or "Bubby Chaya" as her grandchildren say) was born into a world gone mad, a world being torn apart at its seams by warring nations from across the globe. Perhaps the war was not so much about power or territory, but for the very soul of humanity, over the existential question of whether Man must submit to the Will of G-d or may accede to his animalistic impulses. Perhaps the point of conflict was truly over whether or not G-d chose a nation for Himself, or whether He truly wanted a distinct people to guide the world with His light.

But whatever it was that ultimately caused the divergence, Chaya followed in the Abrahamic path of her great ancestor. The world around that little girl soaked up the spilled blood of the innocent. She was raised by gentiles, and all those around her agitated for a greater distance between themselves and their Creator. At the tender age of six, she looked evil squarely in the eye, and knew there was something more, Someone higher. She discovered Hashem on her own, and turned to Him for aid, and a relationship. She swore to Him that if He would be unto her for a G-d, then she would give back by raising more children for His army, and that she and they would continually choose to follow in His ways.

Join us in reading about some of Chaya's life experiences, and hopefully you too will learn that one can always turn to Hashem for aid and a relationship, and that we can always continually choose His path of life.

וּבָחַרְתָּ בַּחַיִּים!
Choose life!

(Deuteronomy 30, 19)

Written the 11th of Sivan, 5783 years from the creation of the world,

Rabbi Shaya Winiarz

(one of those who fulfilled Bubby Chaya's promise)

Preface

This is an important book, written by an important woman, my mother.

The stories told in this book—particularly the horrifying stories of her experiences in the kingdom of the night, the Holocaust—were my mother's milk.

I heard them again and again: the firing squad at the age of five, being buried alive, the baby ripped apart in front of our mother. Sometimes, at the Sabbath meal, there would be a wishbone in the chicken.

Our mother would look at the wishbone and say, "That is how that baby was torn apart." This was the story of our youth, retold again and again in sacred cadence. These stories are but the beginning however for what you are about to read is a tale of redemption and faith. Our mother shows a way to walk from the Kingdom of the night and follow your path to the Dawn. Even as in this world we never fully leave the night behind.

At some point in later life, I began to have a series of mystical experiences—what today are commonly called paranormal—with startling clarity.

They give us direct access to the almost impossible to grasp realization that even what has been ripped apart may somehow come back to together, that torn hearts and broken bodies might yet be stitched back, that as we reweave our bodies, hearts, and souls, the fabric of the broken Cosmos is rewoven in the great Tikkun, the great fixing. This is the ultimate human dignity. We have faith in God. Faith is a memory of the knowing that it is true. And we renew our faith in recovering that memory every day. That is the act of this book, a recover of memory, both of the past but it also implies a memory of the future, a memory of the most beautiful world that we already know is true.

Our masters whose souls were on fire taught us that just as we have faith in God, God has faith in us. God loves us so much he turns to us to heal what the great Kabbalists describe as the Wounded God. In the infinite dignity of healing the Wounded God, our own wounds become whole. For God is always perfect and beyond all wounds, but the very greatness of God is his humility. He allows himself to appear to be wounded for the sake of our healing. This is the essence of the Yiddiskkeit as taught by the greatest of Kabbalistic sages.

The healing of our unimaginably beautiful world—whose insides are lined with love, and yet is at the same time this being ripped apart and broken is the currency of the Divine that moves, drives and even obsesses every fiber of our being. We live in a world filled with broken vessels, broken bodies, broken hearts, and even broken souls—even as the world is unimaginable beautiful. We participate in the healing of our world by moving towards Tikkun—towards wholeness—in ourselves and for the whole. For our personal Tikkun, our personal transformation, is the transformation of the whole.

Publishing my mother's book is a great honor.

This book must be read. It is a book that will change you. Its uncontaminated directness will move your soul and open up all the gates necessary for our own personal journey of liberation, a journey not only to God, but a journey inside of God.

Mordechai Gafni

Prologue

My name is Chaya Bressler Subar. I was born to a well-to-do Jewish family in April 1939, in Nadworna, Poland. I was just six weeks old when my father, Yosef Bressler, was conscripted into the Polish army and left our home. When I was six months old, the Nazis overran most of Poland and the Soviets took control of Nadworna and what was then Eastern Poland.

The next time I saw my father was two years later. My encounter with my father lasted one night and one day. I never saw him again after that.

When I was two-and-a-half years old, my parents made a choice no parent would ever want to make. They gave me up to a family whom they had never met and knew nothing about. They gave me to a Polish Catholic family to hide me from the Nazis. I became a "hidden child," an appellation I would wear for the rest of my life.

I was too young to remember when my father delivered me to the Polish couple, the moment I stopped being Klara Bressler and became Wanja Klimek. But I do remember the Klimeks, righteous people who made the choice to save me at the risk of their own lives.

The Klimeks were Mama and Tatu to me for over four years before my mother, Chana Bressler, came after the war to claim me.

Being a hidden child saved my life. But it also has made my life a challenge I have struggled to navigate.

As I grew up I had no one to validate the truth of what I imagined my experiences were during the years I was hidden. My memories of that part of my childhood begin with the hugs and kisses, the love Mama and Tatu Klimek showered upon me. I also vividly remember the vile curses and repeated beatings I received from the village bullies who believed I was a Jew. Did I actually witness the Nazis storming into our sleepy village and brutalizing our neighbors? Did my five-year- old eyes really see the horrifying sights? And did my ears hear the deafening sounds of their trucks and their murdering machine guns? These memories kept me from falling deeply asleep and haunted my dreams every night of my life until just a few years ago.

I questioned myself constantly: Did I really experience my memories or were they just the stories my mother endlessly repeated to me, reflecting the horrors she had experienced during the war? I had no way of knowing.

After the war, when we lived in New York, my mother had the address of the Klimeks in Poland and she periodically sent them small, well-wrapped packages of clothing, foodstuffs and the few dollars that she could spare. And at one point during my stormy childhood, my exasperated mother threatened to send me back to them. But nothing ever revealed the truth about my life with the Klimeks.

For over 40 years, I kept my history to myself because I felt that no one would believe me. Then on May 26th, 1991, I attended the first ever Conference for Hidden Children. On that day, 1,700 hidden children from 28 countries converged on the New York Marriott Marquis Hotel to find the missing pieces of their lives. Until then, I had never met another hidden child. When I discovered that I wasn't the only one who didn't know if their childhood was real, who were silent about their past, who couldn't trust the validity of their thoughts and feelings, it changed my life. What I remembered almost certainly happened to me. I wasn't crazy.

I attended workshops at the conference in which I learned that multiple marriages, fear of abandonment, workaholism, approval seeking, substance abuse and worse are all common consequences of being a hidden child. I spoke with other hidden children who were still suffering, after more than four decades, the trauma and guilt of surviving a war that most did not survive. Attending this conference and meeting other hidden children unburdened me of decades of uncertainty about myself and empowered me to embrace my past.

Discovering the truth of my history has been a long and often frustrating journey, but filled with surprises. I named my first child Yosef after my father, of blessed memory. Yosef wanted to know about his namesake, but as I had no memory of my father, Yossi became immersed in genealogy. He searched all the Holocaust sites for a Yosef Bressler, but found nothing. How could it be? My father was in the Polish army and then a prisoner of war held by the Germans who, we know, kept meticulous records.

Then Yossi stumbled across a website referencing prisoners of war which cited an Avraham Yosef Bressler. This was my father. His name was not Yosef but Avraham Yosef. For some reason this fact was hidden from me. We were then able to ascertain that if he wasn't killed earlier in a notorious Lublin labor camp, then he was almost certainly murdered in the Majdanek concentration camp not later than November of 1943.

Yossi's interest in genealogy spurred him to locate the gravesite of his paternal great-grandfather who died in Poland. Yossi is a licensed tour guide with many contacts in Poland. In 2017 he planned a trip to Poland with the intent of finding his paternal great-grandfather's burial site. Speaking with his Polish contact, Emil, Yossi told him that his mother had been a hidden child in a small village near Lublin.

Emil responded, "I know that village! I'll see if anyone of the Klimek family from there is still alive." Emil found a first cousin to the woman I called Mama. Her name was Ewa and she was about my age.

I never wanted to return to Poland after my mother and I left so many decades ago. But when I heard that there was someone there who might have known me when I was a child, I agreed to go. Yossi arranged to return to the village where the Klimeks and I had lived and to meet with Ewa.

Yossi learned from Emil that Ewa had a playmate named Wanja Klimek. Yossi asked me, "Did you ever hear of anyone named Wanja Klimek?"

"Yossi, you are speaking to Wanja Klimek!" I exclaimed. However, I did not remember ever playing with a girl named Ewa.

Of course, I was fearful to return to the scene of my worst nightmares. The memories of the abuse and beatings by the neighborhood bullies flooded my consciousness. What if I met those two boys who repeatedly threatened to kill me? I feared they were still living there and would come to finish me off. But the adult side of me was hopeful that I might learn the truth of my past. With much trepidation, I agreed to go with Yossi to Poland, where my father was almost certainly murdered.

My meeting with Ewa, assisted by Emil, an adept translator, confirmed the facts. Yes, the horrifying events, as you will read in my story, actually did happen. I didn't imagine them. This meeting changed my memories from doubt to fact. And for some strange reason, following my reunion with Ewa, the nightmares that had plagued me my entire life ceased. It was a relief to realize I was not going insane after all.

Yossi and I also went to the Majdanek Concentration Camp to stand at the place where my father had been murdered. It was a cold, wintery day when we arrived. I hoped that Yossi would be able to say *Kaddish* there for my father, his grandfather, but it seemed we were the only visitors to the site. We walked around this fearful place and found ourselves standing alone at the enormous pit in which lay the ashes of martyred souls, including my father. Miraculously a group of Jews from Israel approached. Yossi was able, for the first time, to say *Kaddish* with a minyan for the elevation of my father's soul and for all the others who perished there at the hands of the Nazi beast.

Just recently, posted on a Holocaust website, I found a video of my mother, a"h, being interviewed by my cousin Martin. While much of what my mother recalls in the interview is not grounded in fact, the interview sheds light on what life was like for a widowed Jewish survivor who reclaimed her only child after the war. My mother remained haunted by her experiences till her last breath.

My parents' choice to hide me has caused me a lifetime of pain. But it also gave me the gift of life. And with this gift I have the joy that comes from being blessed with children, grandchildren and great-grandchildren of my own. What could be seen as only a source of darkness and negativity can also be seen as a source of light.

Throughout my life I've met many people and experienced many ups and downs. With every encounter and experience, I've had the choice to take the good from it and put the bad in a box, lock it with a key, and deposit it at the back of my consciousness.

I have chosen to tell my story for two reasons. First, I have fulfilled my life-long need to confirm and validate my history. But the more important reason is to show that even in the darkest situations, with the help of G-d we can still make the right choice. The moment G-d puts our soul into a body, he automatically gives us two gifts. First, he enrolls us in a high end university called 'Life.' It is there that we are given the opportunity to practice his second gift to us: the gift and power of making choices. Granted, when we are younger, we have not yet learned how to make choices with wisdom. We often make wrong choices. It is at such times that we have to learn how to take ownership of our decisions, and take responsibility when we make a mistake. Instead of berating ourselves for the mistakes we make, we have to use the gift of choice by realizing we were given an opportunity to learn from the mistake we made, and make a wiser choice. That takes strength. Yes, we can do it!

And walk toward the light.

BEFORE THE HOLOCAUST

Chana Koenig

Members of the Koenig family
(Chana on right)

Chana Koenig

Joseph & Chana Bressler wedding picture, Nadworna, 1936.
All but three people in this photograph perished in the Holocaust

Klara Bressler and her caretakers before she was sent away, May 1941.
Klara is wearing the same coat in the 1945 train station photograph

Chapter 1
Into the Night

Chana heard the knocking. First it was a quiet and furtive knocking. There was something desperate about the sound. She was afraid to get out of bed to answer it. It didn't sound like the Gestapo. They don't knock gently. And besides, the Gestapo was not yet in Nadworna. She started to sweat. Who would be knocking now so late at night? She ran to the door to try to hear voices. The knocking became louder and more urgent. She tried to see out of the window, but the porch was enveloped in darkness. She called out, "Who is it?"

"Me, Yosef, open quickly," the voice pleaded in a loud whisper.

Her pulse quickened.

Yosef slipped into the house with another big, burly man and quickly and quietly closed the door. He embraced Chana, his wife of five years, though they had been apart for most of that time. Yosef was gaunt and looked so much older than his 30 years. His big dark eyes, those eyes that drew her to him, were weary and filled with fear. What had he seen? What would she do to have him back forever? Chana gave them tea from the samovar and what food she could find.

The two men hungrily consumed the small repast, which seemed like a feast to them. The burly man nudged Avraham Yosef. "Get the child. We have to push on."

In 1939, shortly after his conscription into the Polish army, Avraham Yosef Bressler was captured by the Germans and sent to Stalag VIIa, a POW camp in Moosberg, Germany. He was then sent to Stalag VIIb in Lamsdorf in 1940, along with other Jewish Polish POWs. In the winter of 1940/41, he was transferred to the infamous Nazi work camp at 7 Lipowa Street in Lublin, Poland. Within a few months, he made a daring escape to the forest and joined the partisan fighters. That is where he met his travelling companion.

"Chana, this is Paterek" as he motioned to the rough-looking, bearded man to his right. "He knows of a family that is willing to take Klara."

"What? Now? Are you sure? Who are these people? How can we trust them? What should I do?" she said in confusion. Chana looked over to her two-and-a-half year-old daughter sleeping peacefully in the corner of the room.

"Yes, Now. Before daybreak. Get her ready."

Chana packed a small bag with whatever food she could find in the house and a change of clothing, roused Klara from her sleep and dressed her quickly, slipping on her the lovely pink coat she had a seamstress make for her.

Klara, rubbing the sleep from her eyes, looked warily at the big man standing by the door. And she didn't recognize the man who was her father. How could she? The last time she had seen him was when she was an infant.

"Klartchu," Chana explained "you are going on a fun trip with these two men. You'll have such a nice time. This man is your Tatte. You call him Tatte."

Klara had no idea what a Tatte was, but she decided to go with him because he was gentle with soft, big eyes and he caressed her cheek so softly. She liked him. The other one she wasn't so sure of.

Yosef drew close to Chana and begged her to come with him. "How can I leave now? There is no one else but me to take care of the business and the properties," she demurred. Would she regret this, she wondered. "Take the child and find a place for her."

Paterek urged Yosef impatiently, "Let's go. We have a long way in front of us. And with the child, who knows how long it will take us."

Yosef picked up Klara and reluctantly took leave of his Chana, both of them knowing they may never see one another again.

Tragedies and losses were happening so often now in her family. Chana's father, Yisrael Koenig, her saintly, respected and successful father, who had said 'No we don't have to run. This is just a pogrom. It will blow over,' was accosted in Stanislav, a nearby town where he had business. The Gestapo soldier laughingly called out, "Come here Jew!" He grabbed hold of his long beard and cut it to the bone, leaving him to bleed profusely in the street. He somehow made it home to Nadworna to die in his bed shortly later.

And her dear mother, Frieda Koenig. Everyone called her a *tzedekes*, a holy woman. Every Thursday she would cook for the poor, the lonely, the widows and orphans. Chana, who was the third of seven children, would take the brimming jars of soup and meat with kishke, kugels and compote – Shabbos food cooked with love and care – to the poor of Nadworna. She would leave the food on the doorstep, knock and run away so as not to embarrass the recipients.

When Frieda's oldest daughter, Adela, begged her for help with her husband's recovery from the typhus that was raging in the town, how could she refuse? She went without a thought for herself. Her son-in-law recovered, but Frieda caught the dreaded plague and died soon after. As was done with everyone dying from the plague, her holy body was loaded onto a giant wheelbarrow that went from door to door to collect the corpses.

What was left for Chana? Alone in this world of madness. Her parents gone, her siblings scattered, running for their lives, except for Giza, her younger sister. Her husband and daughter torn from her on this dark night. Would she ever see them again? She felt a deep and dark emptiness creep into her heart. Something that was never there before. An emptiness that would never go away.

"How? How, Ribono Shel Olam, could you leave me with nothing?"

Yosef carried Klara until they reached the road leading to the forest. Klara felt safe in Tatte's firm but gentle grip. Though few words were spoken as they walked, whatever Tatte said to Klara felt comforting. When they entered the forest, Yosef finally put Klara down but held her hand tightly. Paterek led the way from there. Paterek's big black beard, heavy black boots and his smell of the forest scared Klara. But she was with Tatte, so it was okay.

The tall trees on each side of the road blocked the moonlight. Klara could only see Tatte, Paterek and the trees. The only sound was from their shoes lightly scraping the gravel path. Suddenly Klara heard trucks somewhere in the distance. Tatte picked up

Klara and ran with her into the forest. Tatte gave her a candy, put his finger to his lips and said, "Shaah!" When they could no longer hear the trucks they returned to the road. One time they heard voices coming from deeper in the forest. Paterek silently pointed to the other side of the road and they ran even faster into the forest. This time they lay down on the ground behind thick bushes beneath the trees. They stayed in the bush a long time after the voices stopped.

They walked several hours down the road through the forest, Klara fast asleep in her Tatte's arms. The morning light woke Klara up. She heard a dog barking and saw a small village just beyond the forest. Klara was hungry, but she didn't cry. Her Mama had taught her not to cry. Paterek was whispering to Tatte. When he stopped he left Tatte and Klara and walked to a little stone house. He knocked on a door. It opened and Paterek talked for a very short time to whomever answered and then turned toward Tatte and motioned him to come.

They entered the little stone house. Tatte held Klara very tightly.

"Her name is Klara Bressler," Tatte said to the man and woman in the little house.

Klara couldn't understand the words the man and woman said, but Tatte said, "Almost three years old."

The lady looked at Klara and smiled at her. She put her arms out to hold the child but Klara turned and buried her face in Tatte's neck.

Tatte said to the lady, "I am a Jew and this is my daughter. From what I've seen, I don't know who will come out of this alive. But at least give my daughter a chance to live. She is yours under one condition. If anyone comes from the family to claim her, you must give her back."

Paterek said to Tatte, "These are good people. They will be good to your daughter. We must go. Now!"

Tatte hugged Klara tightly, and kissed the top of her head for a very long time.

Then Tatte put Klara down, turned around and walked out of the door with Paterek. Klara couldn't see her Tatte's face, only the back of his coat. Klara screamed, "Tatte, Tatte," but he didn't turn around. She tried to run after him, but the lady took hold of her as the man closed the door. Klara continued to cry, "Tatte, Tatte." She broke free of the woman and ran to the door but it was too heavy for her to open. She ran to the window, the only one in the little house, but it was too high for her.

I can still feel his kiss upon my hair. How do I remember this after so many years? That kiss upon my hair. If I close my eyes, I can sense that place on my head. Did I know what was in that kiss? Did I understand what it is to give away a child? That is all I have left of my Tatte. That kiss. I never even knew his name. Only Tatte.

Gone was Klara Bressler. She disappeared into the Polish night. She now became Wanja Klimek. Karolina and Stanislaw Klimek became her new Mama and Tatu. The next day, Karolina took the child to the church in Lublin where she was registered as Wanja Klimek. Klara Bressler was registered on the list of slaughtered Jews. In time, whatever Klara remembered of her mother and father and her home in Nadworna was replaced by the reality of Mama and Tatu Klimek and life in the village. It took some time, but soon the child's previous life faded from her memory and the new family became her only reality.

Chapter 2
Wanja's Trees

The Klimek house had only one room. Its thick stone walls stayed very cool even on the hottest days. When Tatu would come home from his work, his bigness filled up the room. His head almost touched the ceiling. Sometimes he brought Wanja a present from the garden. Once a potato grew that looked like a person with a nose and two funny eyes. Tatu pretended it was a man and made it talk. Mama and Wanja laughed very hard.

  A small wooden table with four wooden chairs stood in the middle of the room. There was only one window in the house. Wanja's bed was under the window. To see out of the window, Wanja had to jump up on the cot's straw mattress and goose-feather quilt. In the far corner Mama and Tatu slept. A dark wooden cabinet contained bedding and another, the dishes and pots. Dug out of the wall near the entrance was a big hole in which Tatu made a wood-burning fire which warmed the house and in which Mama did all the cooking.

  Mama and Tatu went out every day to work their fields. They grew vegetables which they sold in the market on Thursdays.

As Wanja grew older, they left her alone in the house. It wasn't safe any longer for Wanja to play outside, the neighborhood children, especially two older boys, beat her severely. At the age of four, Mama took Wanja to see a doctor due to the severity of the beatings; he advised her to keep her daughter indoors, he didn't think her small body could survive another beating.

Outside the house were two cherry trees. She climbed them easily and ate the sweet cherries before the birds got to them. Sometimes she would stay in her trees for hours at a time. The family called them Wanja's trees. These trees were Wanja's world outside the house.

Every Sunday, Wanja sat between Mama and Tatu in church. She knew her prayers very well. Mama taught them to Wanja at home and she said them every day, not just on Sunday. Mama taught her how to kneel on the hard wooden bench in the church and to bow her head. The Klimeks sat near Aunt Theresa and cousin Ewa. Wanja secretly watched Ewa pray. They were the same age but Ewa seemed to know everything. She was very good at her prayers. Sometimes Ewa turned her head ever so slightly and smiled at Wanja, who always smiled back.

The priest always started his sermon talking slowly and softly while smiling. Then he would start yelling about the *'zhids,'* the Jews, and how terrible they were; how we have to get rid of them because they are filthy vermin – like rats and mice. Wanja didn't like the priest's yelling. She would put her hands over her ears and could feel Mama lean in closer to her. She didn't really understand what he was talking about except she knew that she didn't want to be near a rat. She had seen plenty of them close to the house. *Why would G-d make people who looked like rats?* Wanja thought. Finally the priest stopped his tirade, smiled again and it would be over. They could go out in the sunshine again, away

Chapter 2: Wanja's Trees

from the yelling and images of people who looked like rats.

After church the Klimeks walked home with Wanja in the middle holding hands with Tatu and Mama. Sometimes they would swing her up and she would laugh. If she got tired, Tatu would put her on his shoulders till they got home.

The Wild Ones

One day, when Mama and Tatu were in the fields, Wanja was digging in the dirt in front of the house. Her play was interrupted by the shouts from a gang of boys from the village running down the road. The two biggest, Pawel and Lukasz, had sticks. They were brothers and were the meanest, most hateful of the bunch. They had come by the Klimek house many times before to tease and taunt Wanja. Sometimes they threw things at her and even kicked her.

Mama called them wild ones. "They are nothing but trouble," Mama said.

Wanja stood up as they came closer. She wasn't afraid even though her heart was beating very loudly.

"Go away, wild ones," she yelled in her loudest, five-year-old voice.

They just laughed. The pack of boys surrounded Wanja and started to hit and kick her. Pawel and Lukasz hit her hardest with their sticks and yelled at her, "*Zhid, zhid.*"

Why were they saying 'zhid'? I'm a little girl, not a rat, Wanja wanted to scream. She wouldn't cry in front of them. The boys ran away laughing, leaving Wanja lying in the dirt bruised and bleeding beneath her cherry trees.

When Mama came back from the fields and saw her Wanja

bloodied and bruised, she cried. She wrapped Wanja in a cloak and ran with her to the doctor.

When he saw her, the doctor shook his head and said, "Mrs. Klimek, if you want your daughter to grow up, keep her inside. I don't know how many more beatings like this her little body can take."

So began Wanja's time in the one-room house. Wanja's world had always been outdoors, around the small house, in her cherry trees. There was not much for her to do indoors. She had no toys to play with. She tried to clean the house, but it wasn't something a small five-year-old was very good at. She took potatoes and pretended they were her children, wrapping them in cloth and putting them to bed. She would climb up on the windowsill and watch for Mama and Tatu to come home with the vegetables. When Mama walked in, Wanja ran to her to get the hugs and kisses she loved and needed. She knew that Mama and Tatu would always take care of her, no matter what. Tatu would come in later after tying up the horse and unloading the potatoes and cabbages from the wagon. He would only smile at Wanja, but there were kisses in his smile. She waited all day for Mama and Tatu to come home. So the days passed.

The End of Childhood

One day as Wanja was putting her potato children to bed, the wooden table and chairs in the middle of the room suddenly began to shake. The cups in the cupboard rattled. She thought it was thunder from a giant storm, but there was no rain. She stood on a chair to look out of the window but didn't see anything, but the chair under her wobbled and the roar increased. She was so frightened that she opened the door and ran to her cherry trees. She climbed up as high as she could. The thick green leaves of the tree hid tiny Wanja from sight, but she was able to see down the road, the only road that came into the village.

Six large trucks were barreling into the village, blowing clouds of dust on all sides. Wanja saw soldiers with rifles in each truck. She also saw villagers running away from the road trying to find someplace to hide. Their faces were twisted in fear. She had never seen faces like that before. The trucks came near her house and they stopped. Wanja held her breath so that not even a leaf would shake.

Out of the first truck came two soldiers. They walked up the road. Their boots were shiny and high. They were smiling at each other. They had long guns in their hands. At the side of the road was a mother holding her new baby, wrapped in a blanket. She started to run across the road, looking to get out of the way. To be safe. She didn't see the soldiers coming down the road, smiling, but Wanja did.

The soldiers saw the mother running away from them. They didn't say anything to the mother running with her baby. They just pointed their rifles at her and fired. She fell down still clinging to her baby. Wanja gasped and covered her mouth with both hands to muffle her scream. The mother lay motionless and bloody in the road. The two soldiers walked up to the body. One of them kicked it so hard that it rolled over, revealing the baby. The baby was crying like babies do when they are not near their mama.

Wanja saw the soldiers grinning grotesquely to one another. They both bent down to pick up the baby. One soldier grasped one leg of the baby at its ankle and the other soldier grasped the other ankle. The soldiers walked and pulled in opposite directions. The baby stopped crying.

High up in her cherry trees, surrounded by the green leaves and the blue sky, with her hands over her mouth, Wanja also stopped crying. From that moment on, she decided never to cry again. And never to show anyone that she was afraid. She somehow knew her life depended on it.

Wanja stayed in the trees not knowing what to do. She heard the guns go off a few more times and people screaming and wailing. Soldiers kicked open front doors of houses and walked in. They came out carrying food and whatever else they took. When she couldn't see the dust of the last truck leaving the village, Wanja climbed down from the trees. She went over to where the mama and the baby lay. She picked up the baby and carried her to the yard in the back of the house. In the soft dirt she dug out a hole with her fingers and rested the baby in it. When Tatu came home, she told him what happened and showed him where she had buried the baby. He dug a deep hole a far distance from the house and laid the mother in it. Tatu dug up the baby and laid it gently on top of its mother. He then filled the hole with dirt.

I saw that mother and baby die again and again, that night in my sleep and every night forever.

Wanja was no longer a five-year-old child. She grew into adulthood thinking maybe she never was a child.

The Neighbor Lady

Not long after the soldiers came to the village, the visits from Pawel and Lukacz's mother started one Sunday after church. She knocked on the door and without being invited in, pushed it open ever so slightly and called, "Mrs. Klimek, are you home?"

Chapter 2: Wanja's Trees

Mama startled at her voice, but hid her surprise. "Oh, come in, Mrs. Badjek. How nice of you to visit."

Mama looked at Tatu with widened eyes, as if trying to tell him something. Then she looked at Wanja. Tatu got up and went out of the house, pretending he had something to do.

Mama served her a cup of tea and a cookie. Mrs. Badjek took a bite of her cookie and started to gossip about people in the village. She then cursed the Jews, all the time looking straight at Wanja. When she finished her tirade she gazed around the little house as if looking for something. The door of the dishes cabinet was open and she saw a large pickle jar inside. She walked over to the cabinet and took out the jar, holding it up to admire it. She said, "Mrs. Klimek, this jar is so big. It's just the size I need. Would you mind if I borrowed it?"

Mama, in her sweet way, said, "Of course you may borrow it, Mrs. Badjek."

Mrs. Badjek repeated her visits and her gossip and her cursing the Jews every Sunday after church. And after a cup of tea and a biscuit, she walked out having "borrowed" another item of her fancy. Wanja never liked Mrs. Badjek. And not just because she was the mother of those wild boys.

One Sunday, Mrs. Badjek set her fancy on one of Mama's only two pots. Wanja was standing next to Mama and saw Mama's face fall as she saw Mrs. Badjek eyeing the pot. When Mrs. Badjek picked up the pot, Wanja couldn't take it anymore. She was only six years old, but she understood exactly what was happening. She did not restrain herself from confronting Mrs. Badjek.

"Mrs. Badjek, every Sunday you pick up something that belongs to my Mama and say, "Can I borrow it?" You take it home but you never bring anything back. That's called 'taking,' not 'borrowing'."

Mrs. Badjek didn't like that at all. She looked at Wanja with hatred in her eyes. The same kind of hatred she saw in Pawel's and Lukacz's eyes when they beat her with their sticks, calling her *'zhid.'* But Wanja didn't know just how much Mrs. Badjek hated her. Later that week the Klimeks had a visit that they would never forget. But it wasn't a visit from Mrs. Badjek.

Wanja's Promise

It was lunchtime. Mama was back early from the fields. Wanja was sitting on the windowsill eating a bowl of cold noodles and milk. She heard the roaring of a truck coming up the road. She looked up from her noodles to see it stop close to her house. Soldiers jumped out of the truck. Maybe thirty of them approached the house.

Wanja called out, "Mama, they're coming to shoot me." She didn't know why she knew that, but she did.

They didn't knock on the door. They pushed it open and burst into the house. The crowd of soldiers with their drawn guns and foul smell pushed Wanja and Mama against the back wall. The captain bellowed, "We have it on good authority that she is a Jew," pointing at Wanja. "We've come to exterminate her."

"That's ridiculous," said Mama. "This is my daughter! She is not a Jew. You know we Poles have been helping you kill the Jews. Would I risk my life for a Jew?" Every time she said the word Jew she spit on the ground.

A soldier picked up Wanja and stood her on the windowsill. The captain commanded Wanja, "Say your church prayers out loud."

Chapter 2: Wanja's Trees

Even though her heart was pounding even harder than when she watched the two soldiers murder the mother and her child, she sang her prayers without making a mistake. Suddenly it all came together in her mind. Pawel and Luckaz, the priest, even Mrs. Badjek. And now these soldiers. They were all telling Wanja Klimek that she was a Jew.

The captain pulled Wanja off the windowsill and pushed her against the stone wall. She felt the cold stones against her nose and at the same time, a flow of strength and courage engulfed her. She felt no fear. She wanted to be in her cherry trees, safe and hidden. She wanted to live. With her face pressed against the wall she silently spoke to G-d.

"Dear G-d, please give me the words to get out of this. And I promise you if You let me grow up and get married, if You let me have children, I promise I'll give You back *zhiden*."

Wanja heard the captain shout, "Ready ... Aim." From the corner of her eye she saw guns pointing at her. The captain's hand was up, ready to say 'Fire,' when Wanja turned her head and looked directly in the captain's eyes. She started to laugh and said, "Don't you know you are going to shoot the future generation of Deutschland? What do you think the Fuhrer is going to do to you when he finds out you shot the future generation of Deutschland?"

Mama ran to Wanja and picked her up. She held her tightly. Wanja felt her Mama's heart pounding next to hers. Mama also looked right at the captain and said, "If you're going to shoot my daughter, you'll have to kill us both."

The room became quiet for a moment and for some strange reason, the captain said "Halt!"

The soldiers put down their guns. The captain ordered all his men to leave.

The last one out, the captain, said to Mama, "We are going to Lublin to check the church records. If we find she is a Jew, you'll wish we had shot her. Because then we'll have something much better for her. And for you!"

Wanja lived every day in fear that the captain would come back for her. In that moment, in front of the firing squad, she knew without a doubt that she was a Jew. And that Jews were meant to be killed. But the captain never came back.

Chapter 3
"Lady, don't you want to live?"

Chana Koenig Bressler was always busy with the workers. Even though she was only in her twenties, she assumed full responsibility for her father's farm and business operations. Cooking, supervising, making sure that the workers didn't steal, she didn't have time to breathe. She kept busy to keep from coming near her the fear and worry that was enveloping her Jewish brethren everywhere. Who was left? Yosef never returned after the night he came for Klara. And Klara? Chana had no idea if her daughter was still alive. Only she and Giza, her younger sister, remained.

One morning, one of the maids in the house, Anna Chopta, approached her. *What problem will she bring me now?* thought Chana. This Ukrainian girl was not much of a worker, but Chana couldn't afford to let her go. Not now, when so many of the workers were abandoning their Jewish employers.

"Mrs. Bressler, why are you still here? Don't you know the Germans are in the next town?" warned Anna.

Chana looked at Anna Choptain credulously. *'Where did she*

think I should go? My papers say I'm a Jew!' she thought to herself. '*How could she be so stupid?*'

"What can I do," Chana answered, hiding her impatience. "They'll kill me on the spot if I'm caught. A Jew without an identity card?"

"Lady, don't you want to live?" questioned Anna with dramatic urgency.

Then Anna put her finger to her head. "I have an idea. If all you need are papers, maybe I can help you," replied Anna cunningly.

"What do you mean? How can you help me?" she asked this simple peasant woman whom she had never really trusted.

"It's easy," Anna explained. "I will go to the church and get my birth certificate. Then, I will go to the police and tell them I lost my identity card and they will give me a new one. Then I can give it to you."

"But what about Giza, my younger sister? She's all I have left. I can't leave without her."

"Is that your only problem? My sister would be happy to give up her card and then the two of you can make a run for it."

"You would do that for us?" Chana couldn't understand why this Ukrainian peasant would be so nice to her when other Ukrainians were helping the Nazis, informing on and murdering every Jew they could find. Why would she endanger her life and that of her sister for two Jews?

Anna Chopta adjusted her kerchief and looked around the yard. "Of course I would want to help you out of the goodness of my heart." Anna patted her chest to emphasize her charitable motives. She hesitated a bit before asking her price. "But it will cost you something. After all, our two Ukrainian identity cards could very well save your lives."

Chana waited breathlessly for the price. Her heart was pounding and she prayed that Anna didn't sense her vulnerability.

"It's not so much," Anna continued. "Just your father's house, everything in it and the surrounding acreage. I think that would do it. And anyway, what are you going to do with it? The Germans will take it from you sooner or later," she said matter-of-factly.

Chana nearly fainted when she heard. To give away everything her dear father had worked for all his life. To give it to this Ukrainian peasant woman. Chana thought of the kosher dishes and pots, the *mezuzahs* on the doorposts, the beautiful big hearth and the long table where her family had spent so many joyous Shabbos and Yom Tov meals together. Everything would be hers? This sorrow engulfed her. But she had no time for sadness. She had to be practical. She had to work fast.

"Alright," she acquiesced. "I'll tell my sister and you bring me the papers as soon as you get them."

Two days later, Anna returned with the papers. Chana hid them in the lining of her purse and ran to some address she was given by a friend. In the basement of what looked like an abandoned apartment building, she found a middle-aged Jewish man who was an expert forger. For 100 zlotys each, he made two beautiful Ukrainian passports. Chana was now Anna Chopta and Giza was her sister, Marta Chopta.

Running

The two sisters ran with the clothes on their backs, whatever food they scrounged from the kitchen and all the money Chana had hidden around the house. Chana clutched the purse in the

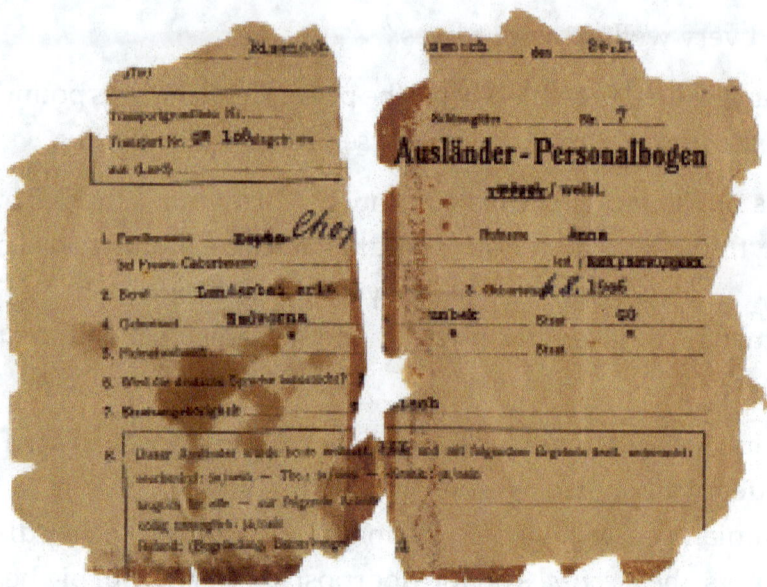

CHANA BRESSLER'S IDENTITY CARD AS ANNA CHOPTA

lining of which she had pinned the address of Klara's foster parents, the Klimeks. Chana and Giza went toward the train station, intent on finding a train going anywhere out of the impending doom which seemed to close in on them from every side.

There were Polish women sitting on the ground near the station, selling carrots, potatoes and cabbages. Chana sat down near them and spread out her skirt to blend in. She hoped no one would notice them. After all, they were well known – Chana and Giza's father had been a wealthy landowner and had been involved in many projects in and around Nadworna. As Chana sat there unobtrusively, pretty and vivacious Giza stood up, her head in the air, hands on her hips, surveying the area, looking a bit too self-confident.

"Giza, sit down. Someone will recognize you," Chana commanded as she tugged at Giza's skirt.

But it was too late. A Polish man, with vengeance in his eyes, came up to her, "*Zhudifka*, what are you doing here?"

Giza answered sweetly, "What are you speaking. I don't understand you. I speak only Ukrainian."

"Come on!" he barked sarcastically. "I remember you from your father's house. You're a Jew and I know it!" He ran off to get German soldiers.

Chana looked up at Giza, fear in her eyes, "I told you to sit down. Now what's going to be?"

The man ran back with two laughing, tipsy German soldiers, each holding a beer stein.

"This one is a Jew!" the Pole declared triumphantly, pointing to Giza. "And that's her sister," he said, looking at Chana.

The young German looked at Giza and remarked to his friend, "Yes, look at her beautiful teeth. Only Jews have teeth like that." He offered her a drink of his beer and Giza said,' thank you' in Ukrainian. Then he offered the stein to Chana who also drank. And then they left, arm in arm. The Polish man ran away, but not before hurling disgusting invectives toward the two sisters.

Chana and Giza ran for the train, hoping to get lost in the crowds. Chana was sure the Germans would come after them, but miraculously nothing happened. They boarded a packed train that was about to leave. Little did they know that the train was headed for Germany. Giza made her way to the front of the train and Chana toward the back, so they shouldn't be seen together. It crossed Chana's mind: Will I ever see Giza again?

Chana was stressed and exhausted and needed to find a place to rest her head. There were no seats and she didn't want to be conspicuous. She didn't have a ticket but hoped that the money she was carrying would buy her safe passage. Leaning against the door between the cars she smoothed the kerchief on her black hair as the gentle rocking of the train lulled her to sleep. Suddenly, the train lurched and she had to grab the door handle to keep from falling over. She steadied herself and looked down. On the floor in front of her she saw something glittering. She looked around to see if anyone else noticed. No one seemed to. She bent down to pick up the shining object and turned toward the door to surreptitiously look at her find.

'G-ttenu!' she exclaimed under her breath. It was a cross on a delicate silver chain. Any other time she would have thrown it down in disgust. But now?

To charade as a Ukrainian woman was one thing. She could easily wear the kerchief, speak Ukrainian like a native and take on all the mannerisms of those peasants with whom she was so familiar. She had supervised so many workers for her father and knew exactly what they were like. But to don a cross of that religion and wear it around her neck? To become a shiksa? This was a betrayal she never thought she would stoop to.

To save her life, yes, she could do it. Without another thought, Chana opened the clasp, put the cross on her neck. Her identity now was complete.

Down the aisle came an official. His conductor's cap spoke for him. His voice, bellowing, "Papers. Prepare your papers and tickets." The passengers started to move about, looking in their rucksacks, taking out papers from pockets. The sleepy train suddenly came alive. A nervous tittering was heard from all sides.

The official was coming closer to Chana. She tried to look as bored and unconcerned as was humanly possible. She grasped her Ukrainian passport and felt her palms sweating. She leaned casually against the door of the train where she was standing. The official came to her. Her heart was beating wildly, yet she smiled sweetly.

"Papers. Tickets," he said in Polish. He eyed her closely. He looked at the passport.

"What's this?" he bellowed. The passengers turned, curious to see if there would soon be some excitement to pass the time.

"This is my passport," Chana said in her best peasant Ukrainian. She showed him the stamp, her picture.

"How much did you pay for this, Jew?"

"How dare you insult me!" she retorted. She reached into her bag and pulled out 600 zlotys. She surreptitiously slipped the wad of bills into his palm.

"I'll be back with trouble for you," he whispered.

The official moved on. "Papers, tickets. Prepare your papers. Tickets."

Chana almost fainted from the tension. She decided to get off the train at the next stop, no matter where she was. She had no choice. She remembered what Anna Chopta had said to her. "Lady, don't you want to live?" Yes, she wanted to live. Even if she had to leave her beloved little sister Giza behind.

Chapter 4
In the Belly of the Beast

Chana stepped off the train as casually as possible, appearing as if she knew exactly where she was and where she was going. She didn't even know what country she was in. Was she still in Poland? She saw a large stand of fir trees close to the tracks. She walked quickly, almost running. She had no luggage to slow her down. She only had a rucksack on her back. Chana made her way toward the densest part of the forest, hoping to find a place to hide and plan for the next couple of days. She would look for berries to supplement the few crusts of bread she had in her pockets.

In the thick of the forest, Chana heard voices. She hid as best she could. There were four girls walking together. They seemed to be running away like she was. Thinking that it would be better to travel with other young women, she emerged from her hiding place and revealed herself to the girls.

"Who are you?" one of the girls asked.

"Anna Chopta," Chana replied in her best Ukrainian accent as if they would somehow recognize her name.

"Why are you here?"

"I got a bit lost. I think I got off at the wrong station," Chana demurred.

"So come with us. We also got off at the wrong station," smiled a girl with short dark hair.

Chana felt a bit safer being in the group. They wandered even deeper into the forest, hoping to stay clear of any soldiers or partisans. Neither would be good for five young women on foot in the forest.

They pooled their food and searched for mushrooms and berries in the surrounding thickets.

As they were wandering in the forest, night approached. In the distance they saw a small wooden cottage that was boarded up and seemed to be empty. One of the girls knocked on the door. A young girl opened the door a crack.

"Please, can we sleep here for the night? We are five girls and we need a place to rest," begged the dark-haired girl.

"Yes, come in," the young girl replied. She went to open the shutter of the window.

"No. No", Chana protested. "Don't open the shutter. Someone might see us."

But it was too late. An old Pole happened by and peered in the window. The girls shrank back into the shadows, but they had been seen.

In less than an hour, they heard the barking of the dogs. Terror engulfed the room. The Nazis had found them and rounded them up outside the cottage. All the young women had papers, except one – the lively girl with the dark hair who had first spoken to Chana. She protested to the soldiers – "I'm a Christian! Don't kill me."

"She's a Jew!" shouted one of the Nazis. "She has dark hair."

They shot her, right there before the eyes of the other young women. Chana gasped in horror.

The girls were taken by truck to the Nazi headquarters and their papers were checked. They were given back the papers. The four remaining young women were to be transferred to Germany to work.

At the offices of the Arbeitsamt, where the girls were to be assigned work, Chana pleaded with the officer in charge. "Please, I am from a village. I don't feel comfortable in the city."

Chana was sent to the farm of Herr Kramer. There she worked milking the cows and helping in the house. She did a very good job and the lady of the house appreciated Chana's work.

One Sunday, Herr Kramer commanded Chana: "Wash the cows today".

Chana stood still, as if she hadn't heard him.

"*Dumkopf,* are you deaf? I said wash the cows in the barn!"

"I can't," protested Chana. "Today is Sunday. My mother taught me I must rest on Sunday. I am a Catholic. I can't work on Sunday!"

Herr Kramer's face reddened with anger. "Do as I say!" he bellowed.

"I won't! Not today."

Herr Kramer stepped closer to Chana. His corpulent cheeks flamed with fury. He took his giant, fleshy hand and grabbed Chana's throat and pinned her against the wall.

"Kill me if you want! I won't work on Sunday," screamed Chana.

Chapter 4: In the Belly of the Beast

As he pulled his hand away, she crumpled to the floor. Herr Kramer left the room, slamming the door behind him. A short while later, the commandant of the Arbeitsamt arrived, obviously perturbed to be disturbed on his Sunday. Chana was brought to him.

"What's the meaning of all this?" accused the commandant, after hearing the story from Herr Kramer.

"I am a Catholic. I won't work on Sunday," cried Chana.

The officer dismissed her.

A few days later, Chana was reassigned to work in a munitions factory. After two weeks, she realized this would be the end of her, because they only gave the workers three potatoes a day to survive on. She wrote two letters to the Arbeitsamt, complaining of the conditions. A few days later, an official came to the factory asking for her.

"You are number 14," he declared.

Chana thought they had found out she was a Jew and that she was being taken to be killed. She put her hands out in front of her, as if to be handcuffed.

"You are number 14," he declared again. "Come with me."

So terrified was Chana that this was her end, her knees turned to jelly. She was put into a truck and taken to Hotel Stern in Ansbach.

Chana was Number 14, the 14th worker at Hotel Stern.

When she entered the lobby of the hotel, there were mirrors all around. All she saw were images of herself. She became afraid. *What has happened to me?* she silently lamented, faced with so many images of herself. *Who am I? I am a Jew. I was a wife. I was a mother. I was a daughter. Now I am this wretched Anna Chopta.*

27

Chana began to cry. The owner of the hotel, Frau Franken, the head of the staff, saw her crying. "Why are you crying? Ukrainian girls don't cry!"

Chana pulled herself together immediately. "No. I am sorry," she said as she wiped her tears. "I am just so tired."

Frau Franken saw that this new girl looked strong and capable. She assigned Chana to be a chambermaid in Hotel Stern, where 48 Luftwaffe officers were stationed! She cleaned, washed laundry and repaired uniforms of the officers. She was working in the belly of the beast.

Chana cleaned every room, but one room she was forbidden to enter. One day Frau Franken ordered her to clean that room. Chana got up on a chair to dust the closet shelf. There she saw a valise with the name stamped on it 'Adolf Hitler.'

The Would-Be Assassin

All at once a compelling purpose seized Chana. "The enemy of my people, the most heinous beast on this earth, Adolf Hitler, may his name be blotted out. He is here," Chana thought. "He must be killed. And I will do it."

Her thoughts raced forward. "But how? I need a revolver. I must have a plan. How can I find a gun?" The ideas swirled in her head for hours and days. She could barely concentrate on her work.

A few days later, Hitler spoke in Ansbach at the Hitlerplatz. Chana stood in the crowds below. The hate within her surged through her body. Her legs nearly buckled as the madman shouted his dream to rid the world of Jews. Struggling to hide her rage, Chana applauded more wildly than the masses that

Chapter 4: In the Belly of the Beast

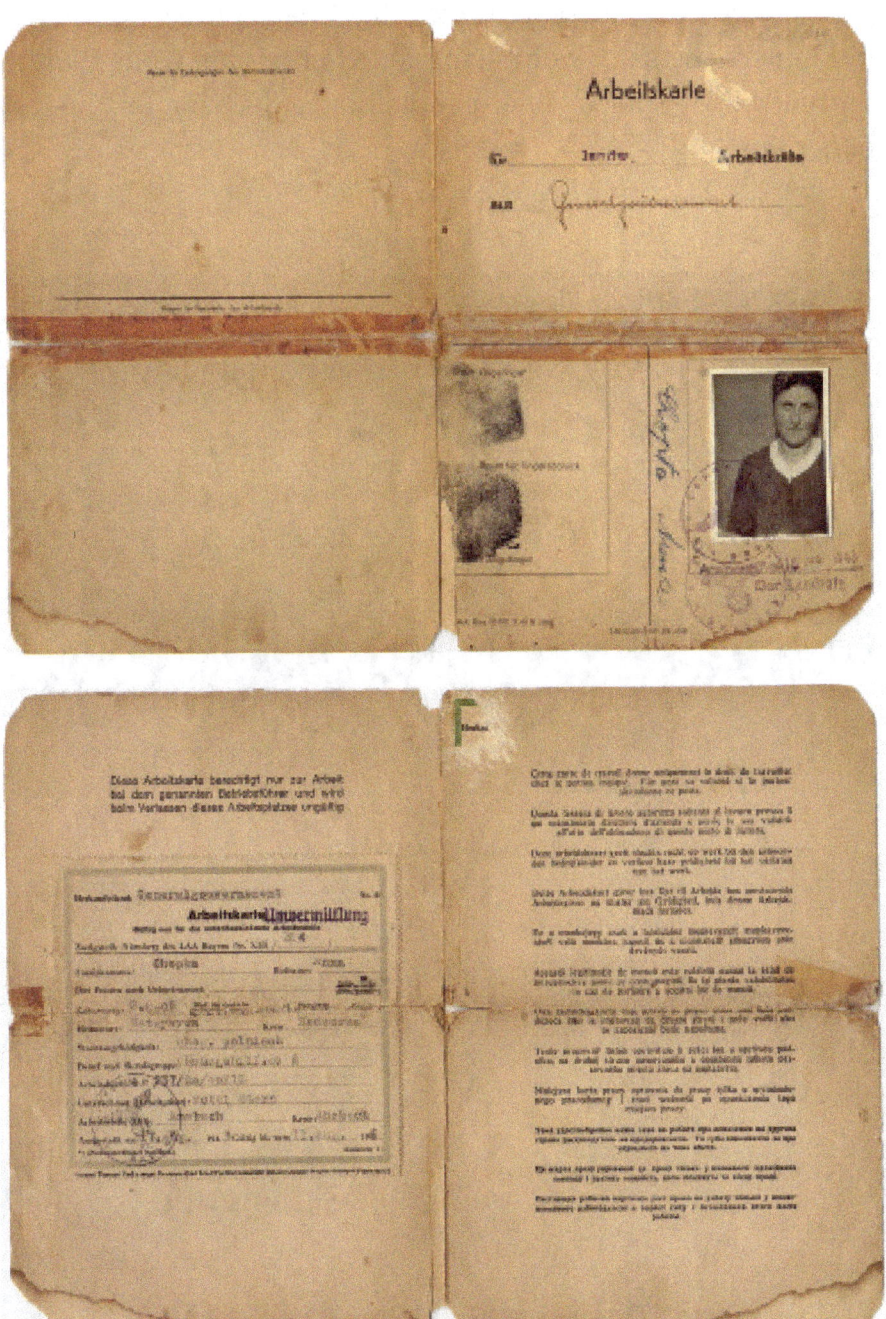

Chana Bressler's forged working papers, August 1943; Anna "Chopta" passed as a Christian and worked at Hotel Stern in Ansbach, Germany surrounded her. She soon realized that Chana Bressler could not kill Hitler. The shame of having failed at her erstwhile plan to murder Hitler and save her people plagued Chana for the rest of her life.

The Hotel Stern in Ansbach, 12.7.1937

Chapter 5
After the War

The war officially ended May 8, 1945. But Jews were still not safe in Eastern Europe. The Jews who survived were terrified to reveal their identities, and rightfully so. Poles, Latvians, and Ukrainians wantonly murdered Jews returning to their homes.

When the Allied forces entered Ansbach, they made Hotel Stern their operating headquarters and officers' residence. Like most Jews, Chana didn't know what to expect from the 'liberators' so she continued to masquerade as Anna Chopta. At one point, a Jewish-American soldier approached Chana and spoke to her in Yiddish. So fearful of being recognized as a Jew, she responded only in Ukrainian.

Though all trappings of the Nazis were removed by the new residents, Chana couldn't erase the images of Nazi men carousing and drinking in the dining room, the lobby and the hallways. She still felt their filthy hands on her the way they grabbed at all the female workers in the hotel. The smell of their vomit on the uniforms she laundered nauseated her. She wanted to run away from Ansbach but she didn't feel safe. So she continued as the trusted worker, senior in her position, who knew the workings of the hotel inside and out.

The Allied officers were different. They treated the hotel workers with respect. They weren't rowdy and crass. They seemed kind and supportive to the Jews they encountered. Chana made herself useful to the American soldiers in ways other than as a seamstress and laundress. Speaking and reading many languages, Chana translated letters and conversations of the locals for the soldiers and she became an indispensable aide to the officers at Hotel Stern.

In time, Chana felt she could risk revealing herself as a Jew. One evening after finishing her shift, she approached the Jewish officer who had once spoken to her in Yiddish. Uncertain how he would respond, Chana stood again, trembling. But this time there was no hate, just hope.

When she said her first words in Yiddish, the officer smiled, interrupted her and said, "You are free now."

Tears filled her eyes and Chana said, "My name is Chana Bressler and I have a daughter that I left in hiding in Poland. I fear I've lost her and I want to find her grave. I have the address of the family who fostered her. Please help me to return there and see what is left of her."

"Mrs. Bressler, we have reports that Jews are being killed by Poles when they try to return to their homes," he warned.

Chana was undeterred and unafraid. The officer understood Chana's need to find her daughter. Though he knew that once she left the hotel she might not return and he would lose a valuable worker, he assigned a soldier and a jeep to carry out her mission.

Chana walked out of the hotel hoping to bury Anna Chopta there forever. Instead Anna Chopta, along with all the death and destruction from which she tried to hide, took up permanent residence in her memory, never allowing her to be the Chana Bressler she once was.

The soldier drove Chana to the German-Polish border. As a repatriated Pole she had access to train travel throughout the country and boarded a train to Lublin. In Lublin, she caught a ride to the stop closest to the Klimeks' village. Chana unpinned from the lining of her purse the small cloth pouch in which she kept the paper with the directions to the Klimeks' village Yosef had written the night he took Klara. The purse with the pouch never left Chana's side for four years. Yosef's paper was her only link to her child. Chana started to walk.

The Door Opens

It was early afternoon when Chana reached the village's only road. With her piece of paper in her hand as she searched for the Klimeks' house, Chana replayed the night Yosef took baby Klara from her arms and ran into the woods. Four years of pain and suffering and death weighed on Chana's heart. She did not believe it possible that Klara was alive.

At the far end of the dusty road, Chana saw a small, stone cottage with smoke rising out of the chimney. A few cherry trees bordered the cottage. This was the house that Yosef described in his note.

Chana's eyes looked down the pathway to the front door. *What if they tell me the Nazis dragged Klara away? Or the Klimeks are murderous Poles and try to kill me?* Chana clutched her purse and headed to the front door. The sweet fragrance of the wild flowers in the forest nearby clashed with the fear and dread that accompanied her. Believing that she could not carry on in life without knowing the fate of Klara, she braced herself for the worst and knocked on the door of the little house.

No one answered. Chana took a deep breath, fixed her eyes straight ahead on the door and knocked again.

The thick wooden door opened but Chana saw no one in front of her. Her eyes dropped down to see a small child, a girl. Was it Klara? How could it be? But yes, this child, her child, was wearing the same pink coat that Chana had sent her away in four years before. The blood drained from Chana's face. She grabbed onto the doorframe to steady herself.

"Lady, are you alright?" asked the child in Polish, alarmed that the woman might fall in a faint before her. "Come in and I will get you a drink."

Chana cautiously entered the small, cramped room. A fire in the fireplace cast shadows on the walls.

The girl poured water into a chipped teacup and placed it on the table before Chana.

"Where is your mother?" Chana asked.

"Mama isn't home, but she'll be back soon with my Tatu."

"Are you alone here?" Chana asked.

"Yes. But I have my kitty who is my best friend." The child pointed to a black cat curled on a little bed.

Seeing the lady's deathly pale complexion, the child was fearful that the woman still might fall over.

"Lady, maybe you need to eat something."

It had been hours since she last ate anything so Chana accepted the child's offer. She brought a slice of crusty dry dark bread and several cherries to the table.

"This is all we have today, but you can have it, Lady."

Chana softened the bread in the water and chewed it slowly.

"What is your name?" she asked the child.

"Wanja Klimek."

Desperately wanting to see if Klara remembered anything of her past, Chana had an idea. When she gave birth to Klara, she didn't have the patience to take care of a crying, needy newborn. She had the estate to manage. Chana's mother, Frieda, stepped in to care for baby Klara. Bubby Frieda only spoke Yiddish to the baby. Chana began to speak Yiddish, hoping it would jar the memory of her past.

Wanja looked at her quizzically. *Why is she speaking these strange words to me?* Wanja thought. She put her hands on her hips, looked up at Chana and challenged, "Lady, do you have a fever?"

"My, my," chided Chana. "You are such a little girl, but you have such a big mouth!"

Wanja laughed. It wasn't the first time someone told her she had a big mouth. And sometimes it got her into trouble. But the trouble was never enough to stop her from expressing herself and saying exactly what she thought.

Wanja said to Chana, "Why don't you lie down and take a rest and when Mama comes back I'll wake you."

Emotionally and physically drained from her journey, and knowing she couldn't leave until the Klimeks return, Chana accepted the invitation. "You can lie down on my bed. It's the one under the window." The black cat jumped off the bed and

Chana lay down, drawing her feet to her chest to fit. She smelled the straw mattress and adjusted her head to avoid the clumps in the pillow.

Two Mothers

A few hours later, Karolina Klimek walked into the cottage. She looked at the woman lying on Wanja's bed and let out a gasp.

She had never seen Wanja's birth mother before, but she instinctively knew it was her. For four years Karolina was haunted by the thought that one day someone may return and try to take away her only beloved child. And now it was happening.

"My G-d, it's Wanja's mother!" she screamed.

Chana woke up with a start. Overcome with emotion she stood up, walked over to Karolina and hugged her.

"No, you are Wanja's mother. You saved her. You are the reason she is still alive."

Both mothers started to cry. Wanja could not understand what was happening. But she knew it was about her.

Chana continued, "But now, I've come to claim my daughter and take her with me. The Nazis killed my husband, my mother and father, my brothers and my sisters. I have no one but her. And I want her back."

Karlolina summoned all her strength and said, simply, "No."

"What do you mean 'no'," retorted Chana. "My husband told me that in case a miracle happens and somebody survives and reclaims her, you have to give her back!"

"Of course I will. When her father comes, I'll give him back his daughter. You, I don't know. I don't know who you are," declared Karolina.

Wanja was hearing all of this as she held tightly on to Tatu. She didn't know what was going on. They were arguing over her. She let go of Tatu and positioned herself between Karolina and Chana. Looking up at both women she asked innocently, "How many Mamas do I have?"

The two women looked down at the girl and stood silent. Chana reached down to touch Wanja's shoulder. Confused by what was happening, Wanja pulled back. Chana withdrew her hand. She realized that her words alone wouldn't get her daughter back. She turned toward the child's bed, picked up her purse and silently walked out of the cottage toward the forest.

Karolina bent down and drew Wanja close, letting hot tears fall onto her cheek.

The Judge Decides

Chana returned to Lublin. She had no recourse but the courts. Her thoughts ran wild in two directions. *Why will a judge listen to me? What does he care about a Jewish mother who has only her daughter left? But I'm a Pole. And I deserve justice from the court. My claim is just.*

She met with Mr. Coleco, a functionary of the courts. He represented Chana before the judge.

"I have two mothers and one child," he explained to the Polish judge.

"Come on Thursday morning with the child and the two mothers," intoned the judge.

News of the case spread quickly. Two mothers and one daughter.

Many spectators came to see the deliberation. Chana's case was the first in Lublin of a Jewish mother claiming the return of her child hidden from the Nazis by a Polish family.

On Thursday morning, Chana appeared at the court. Karolina was already there with Wanja but Stanislaw, her husband, was absent. Wanja kept her gaze on Chana, but didn't let go of Karolina.

The judge directed Karolina to speak first. She stood up and began to cry.

"If she takes the child, it will be too much for my husband. He couldn't even come here today, he was so distraught thinking you would take away his beloved Wanja. I will lose my husband if she takes the child," Karolina sobbed. "This child is everything to us," she pleaded as she caressed Wanja. "The Nazis pointed their guns at my daughter, but I stood in front of them. I did not let them kill her. We risked our lives for Wanja!"

Karolina could not continue. She fell back into her chair weeping, wringing her hands in desperation.

Chana sat through Karolina's impassioned testimony, knowing that the judge's decision would change her life forever. But no emotion stirred within her; she felt cold as stone.

The judge motioned for Chana to speak.

"The Germans did not harm us like the Poles."

Startled by what he had just heard, the judge sternly said to Chana, "Repeat what you just said!"

The judge was visibly displeased but Chana repeated, only louder. "The Germans did not harm us like the Poles.

"I have no mother and father. I have lost my husband and my sisters and brothers. At one time I had a vast estate but traded it all to a worker in my employ for two fake identifications. My husband and I gave our child to these people with the understanding that if any of my family survives, they will have to give her back. I alone survived. And now I want my daughter back."

The judge looked at Karolina. "Did you take the child knowing you might one day have to return her?"

"Yes," Karolina whispered through her sobs.

After an unbearable silence that lasted only moments, the judge solemnly said, "I'm sorry, Mrs. Klimek. Polish law says the child belongs to her birth mother."

Hearing the judge's decision, Chana fainted. Mr. Coleco caught Chana as she collapsed and eased her into a chair.

Karolina's wails and sobs filled the courtroom. "I will lose my husband," she screamed. The silence of the spectators erupted into shouts and cries.

"Silence!" demanded the judge.

The judge was not finished. He ordered Chana to pay the Klimeks 500 US dollars, a virtually impossible sum for a post-war Pole to have in their possession. But she knew that she would not let the judge's ruling keep her from her daughter. Chana turned to the child and in a voice for all to hear she said, "Klara, I will be back for you as soon as I can."

Karolina let go of Wanja and ran to Chana. She pulled on Chana's arm and begged – "Please, Chana, we will find you a place to live near us. Just don't take Wanja away. My husband knows a Jewish man for you to marry. You will start over here. Our lives are nothing without Wanja."

Chana felt gratitude to Karolina and Stanislaw for saving Klara.

But she cared nothing about what would happen to the Klimeks without Klara.

Chana flatly replied, "I have a good job in Germany. I work in a hotel in Ansbach. I have responsibilities there. I must go back. And I will take my daughter."

The judge raised his voice above the clamor and shouted "Silence!"

He then called out, "Wanja, come to my desk."

Still unclear what all the drama in the courtroom meant, she sensed that something important in her life had just changed. The judge motioned to Wanja to come around his desk and stand next to his chair. Everyone in the courtroom leaned forward to hear what the judge was going to say. Pointing to Karolina, he spoke softly to Wanja, "This lady is not your mother anymore." And then he pointed to Chana, "This lady is your real mother. You will have to go with her."

Wanja stood straight, pushed her small shoulders back and retorted in a forceful voice, "If she will take my Mama and Tatu with me, then I will go with her."

Leaving Poland Forever

Chana located one of the many relief agencies that had sprung up in Poland whose mission was to search for hidden Jewish children. She described her situation to the Swiss director of the organization. She presented her identity papers, both genuine and false, the court documents, and the carefully folded yellowed paper with directions to the Klimeks. The director noted all her details and promised to process the claim as quickly as possible. In two days, miraculously, the agency director handed Chana an envelope containing 500 US dollars.

The very next Thursday, Chana returned to the court. Surprised to see Chana so quickly, the judge wrote and signed an order allowing Chana to remove Wanja from the Klimek home. Chana walked out of the courtroom feeling victorious. She had defeated the Poles in court. She wrote out a message telling the Klimeks that she had their money and an order from the judge to take her daughter. They must bring the child with her belongings to the train station on Sunday at noon and she would give them the money. Mr. Coleco arranged to have the message delivered right away.

The Vacation

When Karolina received Chana's message, the deep sorrow that had been dancing around her now gripped her heart. She feared the loss of Wanja would damage her husband's health and rob them of their happiness forever. She didn't know if either of them would survive. She didn't show the message to Stanislaw until Wanja was asleep.

In the darkness she whispered to Stanislaw, "How did she get the money so fast?"

He answered her, "At least we will have the money. The judge did what he could for us to keep Wanja. We have three days before giving up our daughter to that woman."

The next morning, after Stanislaw left for the day, Karolina sat with Wanja after the breakfast dishes were put away. Doing her best to hold back the tears, Karolina told Wanja that on Sunday she and Tatu were going to the train station to meet the lady.

"Are you and Tatu and I going with the lady on the train?"

"No, Wanja. You and the lady are going alone on a vacation."

"What's a vacation, Mama?"

"Oh, you'll go on the train to a place and you will have a very nice time."

"And after that I can come home?"

Karolina put her arms around Wanja, held her tight. "Yes," Karolina lied, tears streaming down her face, "after that you can come home."

On Sunday at noon, Chana paced the platform at the Lublin station anxiously awaiting the Klimeks and Klara. The envelope of US dollars distended her tiny purse. She was anything but calm. This was not a pleasure trip that she was about to take. She had lived four years hiding her Jewish identity as Anna Chopta. She had no one but herself to watch out for. Now she had her

KLARA AT A TRAIN STATION, PROBABLY LUBLIN, POLAND 1945 - NEWLY REUNITED WITH HER MOTHER TRAVELING TO ANSBACH, GERMANY

daughter, but that didn't take away the pain and anger and fear that lived inside her. Chana had survived by shutting out the future and denying the past. The present filled her with anxiety and uncertainty. What would be with her daughter in her life? She felt no joy being a mother once again.

Finally she saw Stanislaw and Wanja at the far end of the station. Stanislaw was holding a small pack in one hand and Wanja's hand in the other. Wanja skipped along happily, her Tatu by her side. Karolina wasn't with them. She couldn't bear coming. She knew that she would not be able to let the lady take her daughter from her and leave forever on the train.

They walked toward Chana who met them with a smile. She wanted to take Wanja's hand but the child would not let go of Stanislaw.

When the station master whistled the fifteen-minute warning to departure, Stanislaw abruptly said to Wanja, "I am going to the kiosk inside to buy some cigars."

He turned toward Chana and she pulled the bulging envelope from her purse and handed it to Stanislaw. He put it under his shirt and turned to go.

Wanja didn't want to be with the lady without him, but Stanislaw resisted her pleas. "You stay with the lady. I will be right back."

Wanja believed her Tatu.

Chana picked up Wanja's pack and said to her daughter, "Come, Klara, let's get on the train and find our seat."

"My name is Wanja. Why do you call me Klara?"

Impatient with the girl, Chana snapped back, "You are my daughter now. Your name is Klara, not Wanja. Come, we don't have much time."

"But where's Tatu? He's coming, too."

Chana firmly took her daughter's hand and turned toward the platform to find their train. "He'll come when he can," she answered.

At a distance down the platform a small group of soldiers was gathered. Chana stood riveted in place, watching the soldiers and trying to make out if they were coming toward her. Something inside her snapped and fear now ruled her. *They know I'm Jewish. They know I have Klara. They want to kill us.* Terrified, Chana grabbed Klara's hand, turned around and ran across the platform to a boxcar on a side rail, pulling Klara behind her.

"Where are we going, Lady?" Wanja yelled.

Chana didn't answer. *We have to hide.* They came to the rail with the boxcar. The boxcar sat just high enough off the rail for Chana to pull Klara with her under it so they could both hide. Chana held Klara flat on the tracks for a full minute. Chana lifted her head off the track just enough to see the soldiers pass by and continue walking far down the platform. When Chana could no longer see them, she cautiously led Klara out from under the train.

"Why did we lie down under that train, Lady?"

Still agitated, Chana looked directly at her daughter and said, "Stop with your questions. We must board the train."

They boarded the train to Ansbach. Chana selected a comfortable booth at the end of the car near the exit. The train whistle announced its departure from the station and the train started to move. Wanja sat up and said to Chana, "Where's Tatu?"

"Sit down and be quiet, Klara. Don't raise your voice on the train. Just sit here and do what I tell you. You are with me now, not Tatu and Mama."

From the sharp tone of the lady's voice, Wanja understood that she had better do exactly what the lady told her. At least until she returned to her Tatu and Mama.

After some time sitting silently with Klara beside her, Chana heard boisterous voices enter through the door at the opposite end, interrupting the quiet hum of the passengers in the car. She looked up to see soldiers on leave with beer bottles in hand. She looked around to see her seatmates asleep and abruptly picked up Wanja and pushed her into the luggage compartment opposite their booth. Chana closed the compartment door, leaving Wanja in the dark cubicle. The child stayed squashed deep inside among the valises and bags until the soldiers passed to the next car. Soldiers passed back and forth several times during the trip and each time, Chana hid her daughter in the baggage compartment.

Wanja thought, *I don't think I like this thing called a vacation.*

She was miserable, crying and whining. It was the first time in four years that she had been separated from her Mama and Tatu. And now she was with this lady who threw her under a train and inside a dark luggage compartment. She began to feel ill. Her stomach hurt and she was unable to keep anything down. By the time they got to Ansbach Klara was a very sick child.

Chapter 6
Ansbach

Klara's strength returned after several days of bed rest and hot meals, courtesy of the hotel. The American commander was surprised and delighted to have Chana back.

Chana rented a small room for the two of them, a short distance from Hotel Stern. It was in an apartment of an old, elf-like woman. She had a sweet smile, ruddy cheeks and many cats. She had no children of her own and was very warm and loving toward Wanja, who called her 'Wulfela.'

Chana resumed laundering towels and linens and repairing army uniforms. The commander again had her translating documents and interpreting the locals. She quickly settled back into her prior routines, leaving Klara with many hours to herself. Klara spent the day mostly sitting alone on the front porch of the hotel watching and listening to the noisy rushing traffic on the street. She had never been in a town as large as Ansbach. The many buildings and the bustle of the street fascinated her. Occasionally she saw young children her age walking to and from school by themselves.

Chapter 6: Ansbach

Every morning Chana and Klara walked together from where they roomed to the Hotel Stern. Klara paid attention to the sights and signposts along the way.

One morning Klara said to Chana, "I don't feel so good today. I want to stay in bed. I know how to walk to the hotel. Maybe later when I feel better I'll come to meet you."

Just as well, Chana thought. *I won't have to keep an eye on her; one less thing for me to do at the hotel this morning.*

"Don't get lost. I have too much to do today and can't leave the hotel to look for you."

Excited to be free of the lady so she could explore Ansbach, Wanja waited just long enough for Chana to be out of sight and quickly dressed. She knew how to be alone and how to entertain herself from the long hours she spent alone waiting for Mama and Tatu to return from work in the field.

She put some crackers in a bag and started down the street toward the hotel. *Today I'm going to see what I want to see,* she said out loud to herself. At the first intersecting street, Wanja turned left, away from the direction of the hotel. She walked wide-eyed, energized by the cool morning air and the sound of the birds chirping in the trees along the street.

She didn't know where it would lead, but she didn't care. *When I get to where I'm going I'll just turn around and come back the way I came. I won't get lost and the lady won't have to look for me,* Klara assured herself.

As she walked she thought, *I miss Tatu and Mama. But I like this kind of vacation I'm having now.* Her thoughts were interrupted when she heard singing coming from an old, run-down apartment building just ahead of her. The singing drew Wanja closer. She stood beneath the window to hear better, but the words didn't sound like any words she had ever heard. *It's not Polish. And doesn't sound like what the soldiers speak at the hotel. And it's not German either,* she thought. But the words didn't matter. The melody was hauntingly beautiful, calling to her, reaching the *neshama* deep within her.

The windows were too high for her to see who was singing, so she walked through the iron gate leading to a dark hallway in the building.

At the far end of the hallway light shone through an open door. She quietly tiptoed toward the light. She stood in the darkness, peeked in and saw a group of old men. She counted eleven of them. Each one was wrapped in a black and white striped cloth with strings hanging from it. They all stood with their back to the door facing an open cabinet at the front of the room. One man stood in front of the cabinet facing the others, holding something heavy in his arms. It was wrapped in a colorful cloth and had two wooden poles sticking out of it. As they sang, the men swayed from side to side allowing Wanja to see a small black box crowning each man's forehead and a black strap holding another small black box tightly wound around one arm. She was transfixed at the sight and sound of these old men, singing and swaying. Unaware of her own movement, she was drawn through the door and now stood inside the room.

One of the men saw the child, motioned to her and said in Polish, "Come here, little girl."

The man had a warm, gentle smile. He was standing next to a table against a side wall. When Klara came near him he picked her up and put her on the table. "What is your name?" he gently asked.

"Wanja Klimek," she sang out, confidently, smiling. And then she thought better and said, "But some people call me Klara Bressler."

"Very nice. Let's just call you Klara Bressler. That's a nice Jewish name."

"And what are you doing here, Klara?" he continued.

"I'm on a vacation with a lady," came her reply.

"Very nice."

The old men treated her kindly. They gave her sweets and invited her to return whenever she wanted.

For the next two weeks, Klara made every excuse she could to avoid walking with Chana to the hotel in the morning. Chana was only too happy to accept the child's excuses, leaving her free of caring for the girl. Chana was discovering that having a six-year-old girl in tow was disturbing her well-managed routines.

Happy to be free of the lady, Klara ran to the building each morning to be with the eleven gentlemen singing their hypnotic melodies. She was captivated by the singing and the warmth of the old men. Besides the sweets they showered on her, she was excited to learn the Yiddish words they spoke to her. It was like speaking a secret language. She was intrigued by the books with the funny black squiggles in them that the men sang from.

One morning, after the singing, one of the men took her by the hand and led her to the far end of the room. In the corner leaning against the wall was a scooter nailed together from three pieces of unfinished wood. The man said to Klara, "Do you know how to ride it?"

Without hesitation Klara put her hands on the rough handle-bars and her right foot on the base. Overjoyed, she circled the small room until the man stopped her and said, "I made this for you, Klara, so you can get here more quickly in the morning."

"*A groise dank,*" beamed Klara. This scooter was the first toy she had ever owned.

You're not Wanja Klimek

Klara loved her time with the old men but she yearned to go home. She needed Mama and Tatu's hugs and kisses. There were no hugs or kisses, in fact no warmth at all from the lady. One day in their room, Klara politely said to Chana, "Thank you, Lady, for this vacation and now I want to go home."

Chana looked disbelievingly at Klara, grasped both her tiny arms, picked her up and roughly sat her on a chair.

"All that I've gone through to save you and this is the thanks I get!" Her voice reached a feverish pitch.

"I told you at the train station in Lublin you are not Wanja Klimek. Your name is Klara Bressler and I am your mother. You heard the judge. He told you I am your mother, not Karolina Klimek."

"No, no," Klara cried. "I want my Mama and Tatu. They love me and are good to me."

Chana did not know what to say or do. She wanted to shake some sense into this ungrateful six-year-old. Unable to stem her burning anger she said the words that were enough to scar Klara's six-year-old heart. "You are never going back to those people!"

The Diagnosis

Within a day after hearing the brutal message Chana gave her daughter, Klara became listless, lost all color in her cheeks and began to cough incessantly. She wouldn't eat. Her limp, little body lay in bed, nearly lifeless. Terrified that her daughter would die, Chana brought Klara to a sanatorium for an evaluation.

(L TO R): CHANA BRESSLER, KLARA, REUNITED WITH CHANA'S SISTER, GIZA; OCTOBER 3, 1946, ANSBACH

(L TO R): FRIEND, KLARA, HER MOTHER AND GIZA; ANSBACH

After extensive testing, the doctor reported to Chana. "Mrs. Bressler, I am sorry to tell you that your daughter has developed spots on her lungs, a precursor to tuberculosis. I don't believe she has more than six months to live."

No, thought Chana; *they can't take Klara, too. I will be left with nothing but death and darkness.* Chana took the sick child back to their small room and ran quickly to Hotel Stern where she had access to fresh food. She fed Klara real butter, whole milk, fresh eggs and rhubarb. It took a few months until the coughing ceased and Klara's colorless cheeks turned pink. Klara regained her full energy and Chana quieted the dark fears of death and destruction that threatened her heart and mind.

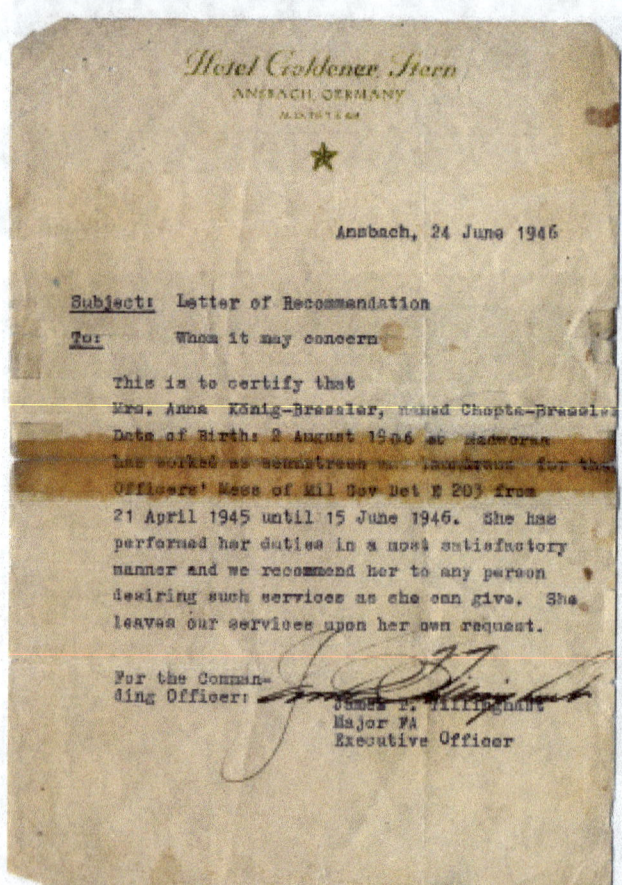

LETTER OF RECOMMENDATION FOR CHANA BRESSLER FROM U.S. ARMY, 1946

Chapter 7

The Long Road Out

In 1945, Chana made an application to immigrate to America. She waited two years before receiving notice that she and Klara were eligible under the 75,000 per year quota system for Jews. All they needed was a physical exam reporting a clean bill of health. Chana passed; not Klara. There were still spots on her lungs. The application was rejected.

Chana heard from someone that one could reapply in another city and perhaps have better luck. So Chana and Klara moved to the American-Occupied Zone in Stuttgart. Chana rented a room in a house owned by a

Klara in Germany

CHANA, KLARA AND GIZA

SCHOOLGIRL KLARA IN STUTTGART

kindly couple, Mr. and Mrs. Adam. The house was well kept and had a large flower and vegetable garden.

Chana reapplied for immigration to the United States and waited. She enrolled Klara in the elementary school in Stuttgart's Displaced Persons Camp. Klara also attended a Jewish school in the DP camp where she learned the *aleph-beis* in Hebrew. Chana honed her skills as a seamstress in the ORT School at the camp.

Klara's first introduction to America came in the DP Camp in Stuttgart. A lady came to visit the children in the school. She was from America and was very pretty. She was wearing a dress that was so fancy, so unusual that Klara could not stop staring at it. The dress was a lovely light beige color and from the hem up for perhaps six or eight inches were decorative buttons! They were in varying sizes and shades of light brown and dark brown.

Chapter 7: The Long Road Out

Goodness, Klara thought, *how could she have so many buttons?* (It was almost impossible to find a button or needle and thread in the camp.) It was so stunning to this little girl, who had been told so many times about America, the *Goldene Medina*.

The stunning dress so impressed Klara, she said to herself, "This dress with so many buttons is *taka* America! This is the *Goldene Medina* everyone talks about. In the *Goldene Medina* there is so much of everything I can even have buttons all over my dress."

CHANA

CHANA AND KLARA (LEFT), GIZA (SECOND FROM RIGHT); GERMANY

Another year passed and Chana still had not received word of her application. It was now four years since she had first tried to leave blood-soaked Europe, but her desire to go to America hadn't weakened. In case it couldn't be, she had a backup plan. Her best friend from childhood, Pepi, had immigrated with her husband to Israel. If all else failed and she could not immigrate to America, she and Klara would live near Pepi in Haifa and work with Pepi's husband who sold flowers on street corners. He did quite well, so she heard. But Israel was only a "last resort" option to Chana.

She searched for another route to America that could bypass the painfully long wait for Immigration Department papers under the quota. She learned that an American citizen could sponsor a relative who survived the war in Europe, and that relative would be processed outside the immigration quota. Chana's brother, Max, lived in America. He had left Europe for America fifteen years earlier. With the outbreak of the war, he and Chana lost touch with one another. But somehow she would find Max and he would be their sponsor, Chana planned. She was given the name of a lawyer in New York who connected survivors with family in America.

She wrote to the lawyer and asked him to help her find her brother. He agreed. The lawyer asked Chana for Max Koenig's address, but all she remembered was "The Bronx." The lawyer was not deterred. This was not the first time he would begin searching for a relative without an address.

The lawyer called all the Max Koenigs in the Bronx phone book and asked each one, "Do you have family in Europe?" Eleven times in a row he heard "no." But on his twelfth call he reached a Max Koenig who said, "Yes, I had a large family in Europe, but they were all killed in the war."

Chapter 7: The Long Road Out

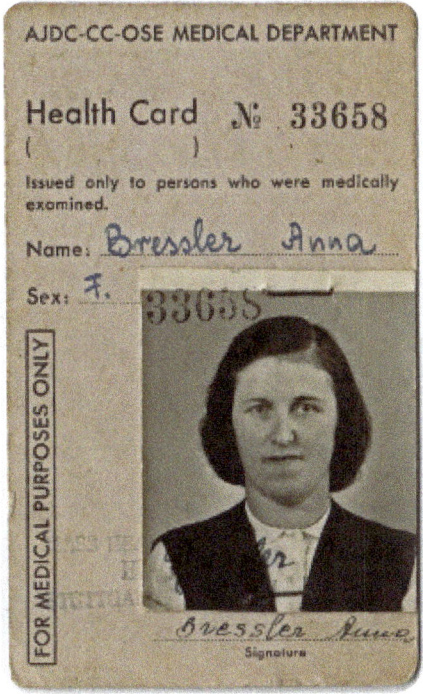
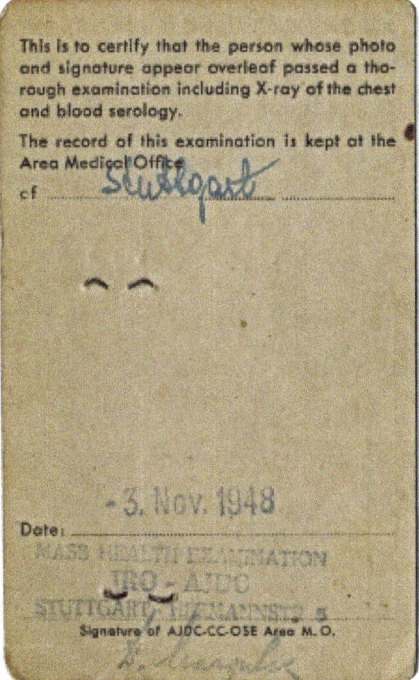
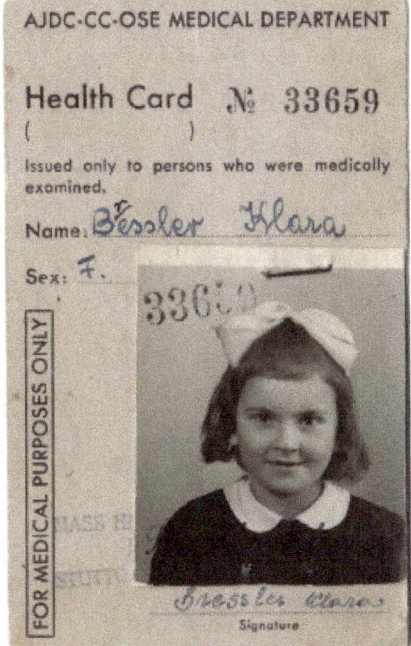

IRO/AJDC (International Refugee Organization/American Joint distribution Committee) Health Card for Anna & Klara Stuttgart, Germany, November 3, 1948

"Could it be that you had two sisters, Chana and Giza?" the lawyer asked.

"I did, but they are dead."

"Well, Mr. Koenig, I am happy to tell you that they are not dead. They are both alive and living in Germany. Your sister Chana has a young daughter and they all want to come to America. And they can with your help."

MAX KOENIG, 1930s

With the lawyer's guidance, Max Koenig went to HIAS, the Hebrew Immigrant Aid Society, and applied to sponsor his two sisters and niece.

Chana and Klara were soon to leave Germany and come to America. Giza and her husband, Sam Horowitz, whom she married after the war, remained in Ansbach and would follow later.

Chana's perseverance was finally rewarded. In mid-January 1949, Chana received a notice from HIAS that she and Klara could immigrate to America under the sponsorship of her brother, Max Koenig. Chana's perseverance was finally rewarded. There was space for them on a ship transporting displaced persons leaving Bremerhaven on February 1st.

Finally Leaving

Chana showed the notice to Klara and said, "We are going to America. My brother, your Uncle Max, arranged for us to come to him in New York. We will be leaving Germany on a ship that will go across the Atlantic Ocean and take us to America. The ship leaves in two weeks."

Klara was excited. Her imagination ran wild thinking about what she could see and do in the *Goldene Medina*. Her spirit for adventure was piqued thinking about crossing the gigantic Atlantic Ocean.

Chana and Klara packed everything they owned. Early in the morning on January 31st, as they were about to leave for the train to Bremerhaven, Klara said to her mother, "I want to take my scooter that the nice man in Ansbach made for me."

Chana said, "You can't take it. There isn't a place where you can ride it on the ship. And it is just another thing we have to carry." Klara wasn't happy to leave her special gift behind, but she did as she was told and gave the scooter to a friend in Stuttgart.

At the train station they met the representative from HIAS who assisted them to board the train. Klara saw children, both younger and older than she, who were also being helped to board the train with their parents. Some families had lots of suitcases and bundles and some carried only one or two. Chana and Klara managed to find seats that had room enough for all their baggage.

The train ride to Bremerhaven took about eight hours. They arrived in the late afternoon and were taken by another HIAS representative directly to the Emigrant Staging Area at the Bremerhaven harbor. There they presented their papers and were told to board the ship.

Klara had never seen a harbor nor been on a boat. The salty smell of the ocean was something new to her. And every activity around the boat grabbed her attention. To nine-year-old Klara she was once again on an exciting vacation adventure.

She was awed by the size of the ship. It looked to her like it could carry a whole village of people. In fact, it could. They boarded the USS Marine Flasher, a ship that was constructed in 1945 as a US military troop carrier fitted to transport up to 3,500 soldiers and their gear. After the war it was commissioned to bring displaced persons from Germany to America. On this mission there would be nearly 600 emigrants.

USS MARINE FLASHER

Crossing the Atlantic

The accommodations on the ship were minimal. From the top deck of the ship they climbed down a steep circular metal staircase to a large lighted room filled with tables and benches. A steward standing at the bottom of the stairs spoke to them in English. When it became obvious to him that Chana and Klara didn't understand him, he gestured with his hands feeding himself and then pointed to the inside of the room. They understood that this was the dining area. He directed them to another circular staircase at the far end of the dining hall and put his two hands together against his cheek, to say that's where you go to go to sleep.

At the bottom of the second staircase stood another steward. He greeted them with a friendly smile, pointed to his chest and said, "Shnappsie."

He smiled at Klara and pointed to her as if to ask her name. Klara looked at him quizzically but didn't respond. Again he smiled and again pointed at his chest and said, "Shnappsie."

Chapter 7: The Long Road Out

Klara liked his smile. In fact it was the first smile she had seen on anybody since they left Stuttgart. She caught on to what the steward was saying and pointed to herself and said, "Klara."

Shnappsie smiled again, reached into a sack at his feet, pulled out an orange and handed it to Klara. With a big, warm smile he pointed to her and said, "Klara." Again he pointed to himself, said "Shnappsie" and tipped his sailor cap to Klara.

Klara smiled a big smile, pointed to the steward and said, "Shnappsie." She then pointed to herself and said, "Klara" and curtsied slightly. She held the orange to her nose to smell its juicy aroma, lifted her eyes and said, *"Danke."*

As they came to the entrance of the sleeping area, Klara turned around waving the orange in her hand and called out, "Shnappsie." Shnappsie looked up, beamed his big smile, waved his hand and called "Klara." Klara had a friend.

Chana and Klara found a cot and a hammock next to each other against a back wall. It was a long walk to the latrines but at least no one was next to them on one side. Klara liked the idea of sleeping in the hammock. When she climbed in to try it out, she made it swing from side to side. "This is going to be fun," she said to Chana. She would soon discover what kind of fun it would be.

The room filled up with people. All 600 passengers were in this one room. The noise level rose quickly. Babies were crying, metal cots clanging. The roar of the ship's engines was constant in the background. People were yelling to each other in order to be heard.

The smell of all the people in the room quickly became heavy. Latrine facilities at the opposite end of the room added their strong, unpleasant odor. The air in the room was thick.

Klara wanted to go outside, but Chana wouldn't let her go by herself. Already the combination of noise, poor air, and gentle motion of the ship still at dock made Chana feel queasy. She did not want to go anywhere off her cot at the moment.

A steward entered the room and rang a large bell. The room silenced and he called out in Polish and German, "Dinner." The room began to empty but Chana didn't feel well and didn't want to go upstairs to eat. Klara said, "That's okay. I'll eat my orange."

Klara was lying in her hammock later that night when one long blast of the ship's horn signaled that the ship was leaving the dock. Klara's hammock swayed gently from side to side as the ship began to move. She was so excited to finally be leaving that she didn't smell the heavy air, or hear the babies crying or the roar of the ship engines. *This is a real vacation,* she thought. *I'm going to the Goldene Medina.*

Throughout the night and all the first day of the voyage Chana felt nauseous and didn't get off her cot. Klara, too, began to feel the effect of the ship's motion. She had never experienced the kind of swaying and rocking motion that comes with crossing the ocean. A new noise penetrated the din and a new smell filled the room. People retching increased throughout the night and day. Klara's hammock swayed more forcefully. She, too, didn't want to eat anything.

No announcement was made to the passengers, but the USS Marine Flasher began sailing across the Atlantic into a violent winter storm. As the storm intensified, nearly every passenger became ill. By the third day at sea almost every passenger was in bed, too sick to move. Chana and Klara had no desire to eat. They sipped water and only left their beds to run to the latrine to relieve their seasickness.

Chapter 7: The Long Road Out

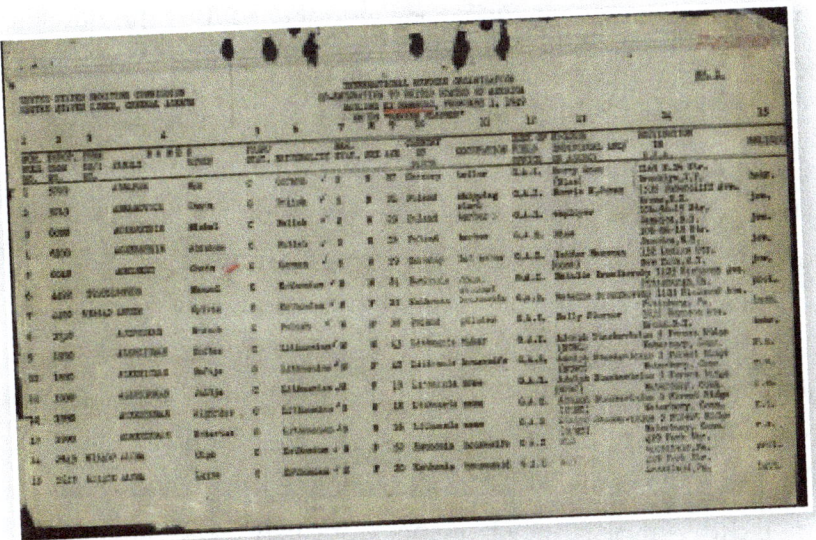

Pages from the Manifest of the Marine Flasher

Word spread among the passengers that there were not enough lifeboats for everyone if something were to happen to the ship in the storm. Very few aboard, if any, except for the crew, had ever been on the ocean. Murmurs of fear were heard. But the nausea and general malaise of everyone kept them pacified. Not many passengers had the strength to complain.

The storm continued for many days. But Chana and Klara were saved from dehydration by a gift from Shnappsie, Klara's friend. One evening, Klara was dozing in her hammock and heard someone call her name. She rolled over and saw Shnappsie standing there smiling his warm smile at her. In his hand was a sack which he opened into her hammock. Oranges fell out. He took one, peeled it and handed it to Klara. He motioned to her to eat it. She held the peeled orange and smelled its fruity fragrance. The smell didn't nauseate her so she cautiously took a small bite. The citrus flavor tasted good. The juice and the pulp perked her up and went down easily. She put the rest of the slice in her mouth and chewed it quickly. She took off another section and smiled a weak but grateful smile to Shnappsie before devouring it. Shnappsie the sailor knew what calms a seasick stomach. The next day Shnappsie came by again with more oranges for Klara. She took some and then gestured to him to give oranges to the people in the cots and hammocks next to hers.

On the eighth day, the seas settled down and the trip became bearable. It was a full seven days from the start of their journey before Chana and Klara felt well enough to venture up to the top deck. People were everywhere. Some were walking around the deck; others sitting on their suitcases or bundles; still others parked at the railing looking out at the endless sea. Klara wanted to stand at the rail. They found a space for the two of them toward the front of the ship. Silently they each stood looking ahead, the cold sea breeze chilling their faces.

Chapter 7: The Long Road Out

Chana's thoughts turned back to her mother and father and their brutal treatment by the Nazis. She pictured the family house with its ornate dark wood furniture, flowery china dishes and silver cutlery. Her mind's eye scanned the fertile fields the family owned. She heard Anna Chopta saying "Of course, it will cost you something" and how devastated and desperate Chana felt giving her the entire estate for the forged identity papers. She saw Yosef's deep brown eyes and felt his strong arms around her and sensed his despair as she handed Klara to him to hide with the Klimeks. How deeply she yearned to be with him. She couldn't block out reliving the crass calls and filthy hands of the Nazi officers at the Stern Hotel.

Please, sea, Chana silently begged, *free me from the pain in my heart. Take away these pictures and sounds that constantly plague me.*

Klara's heart was soaring. She had never felt the wind blowing so strong against her face as she did now. As the ship bounced up and down cutting across the waves, Klara felt she was flying. She didn't know what she would see in the *Goldene Medina,* but given how free and alive she now felt, she believed absolutely that everything there would be beautiful.

On the eleventh day of the voyage Klara heard that the ship would soon be in America. She begged Chana to let her go on deck to see America. Chana agreed and Klara went up on deck and stayed up all night, watching the lights in the distance get brighter. Klara became mesmerized by lights which flashed green, yellow, red over and over again. She had no idea what the lights were for, but their endless repetition said to Klara that wonders awaited her.

On February 11, 1949, the USS Marine Flasher arrived in Boston Harbor. Chana and Klara Bressler were finally in the *Goldene Medina.*

Chapter 8
AMERICA!

Max met Chana and Klara at the boat. Chana was an unmarried young woman when Max left Poland to make a life in America. Max would have been killed in the war like the rest of the Koenig brothers, if it wasn't for his wife Anna. Anna's family was from Solotwina. She had been living in America and had become a citizen. She was engaged to a boy from there. But when the *chassan* broke the engagement, a devastated Anna returned to Poland to recuperate from her bitter disappointment. There she met handsome and rich Max. They fell in love and soon had a big wedding in Nadworna. In 1933 they returned to America, hoping to make their fortune and start a family.

Max and Chana had exchanged letters up until the war began, but then the letters from Chana stopped. The news from Europe left Max with little hope he'd ever see Chana or any of his family again. He believed it was a miracle that he was now standing with his younger sister, Chanaleh. And Klara! Max showered Klara with smiles and kisses on her head. He was so thankful to be "Uncle Max," a title he had given up ever expecting to hold.

Chapter 8: America!

Klara took to Uncle Max right away. She loved the attention he paid her.

With Max to translate for them, Chana and Klara passed through immigration and customs with little difficulty. From the harbor they went by taxi to the train station. What immediately caught Klara's attention on the street were the traffic lights which turned from green to yellow to red and green again.

"Uncle Max," Klara exclaimed, "I saw these lights from the ship. They were so pretty and they kept going on and off and on and off. I see the cars stop and go with them. Is that what they do? I thought they were just to make everything look pretty." Klara was wide-eyed and excited by everything she saw in the big, busy American city.

But there was one thing she hadn't seen yet in the *Goldene Medina* – the gold. In the DP camp Klara heard that in the *Goldene Medina* the streets were paved with gold, but she didn't see any in Boston. They rode the train from Boston to New York. Klara insisted on a window seat so she wouldn't miss seeing the gold along the way. The train passed through towns, farmland and forests but Klara saw no gold.

Maybe when we get to the Bronx, where Uncle Max lives, we'll see the gold, Klara thought.

When they got to the Bronx, what Klara did see were giant buildings, people everywhere, traffic jams and dirt. She never saw so much dirt in the streets. *Doesn't anyone sweep up around here?* she wondered.

When they finally pulled up to Uncle Max's apartment on Cypress Avenue, Klara couldn't keep it inside any longer and asked, "Where is the gold, Uncle Max?" Uncle Max just laughed and proudly showed them his children's shoe store, which was right next door to his home.

MAX AND ANNA'S WEDDING; NADWORNA, 1933

"This is where my gold is, Klara. I sell shoes for children. That's how I get my gold. In the *Goldene Medina* you can find all the gold you want, but you have to work for it. Remember that, Klara."

Max and his wife, Anna, tried their best to welcome their long-lost relatives. Max rented Chana and Klara a room across the street from his store so they would feel close to his family. Max and Anna had two children: Martin who was about Klara's age, and Barbara, a couple of years younger. Max and Anna hoped the cousins would get along well.

Typical of children their age, Klara and Martin were cautious about interacting with one another. Klara spoke no English and Martin spoke no Yiddish, so they couldn't talk to one another. The only thing Klara could say to Martin that he understood was *gai shlufen* (go to sleep), but to Martin those weren't friendly words. Also, Martin wasn't happy that his father paid so much attention to Klara when she was in their house. Martin was too young to understand how his father felt about having his sister again and being able to help her and Klara rebuild their scarred lives. No matter what Max and Anna did to encourage the relationship, Klara never became friends with Martin and Barbara. It hurt Klara deeply that her cousins didn't accept her, because she yearned to be part of a family. Her cousins couldn't understand or relate to Klara or her feelings.

Public School

Chana enrolled Klara in the local public elementary school. Chana and Klara arrived at the school very early in the morning to meet the principal but she wasn't there yet. While they waited outside her office Klara looked all around her and tried to understand what she saw. The hallway leading to the principal's office had a showcase on one side in which were gold, silver and bronze medals and statues of men and women running, jumping and holding balls.

She asked Chana, "Is this the school's gold?"

The principal arrived and invited Chana and Klara into her office. Chana had difficulty with English but was able to make herself understood. Klara understood nothing of what her mother and the principal were saying. Klara kept hearing the principal say "Claire" and pointing or nodding toward her. Chana explained to Klara that the principal wanted to give her an American name so that the children in the school would be friendly to her.

Klara said to her mother, "I like my name Klara, but if it's better to be Claire in school, okay."

The principal stood up, motioned with her hand to Klara to come with her, and said, "Come Claire. Let's go to your class."

Chana said to Klara, "You will be fine here, Klara." And Chana left the school. As Klara walked down the hallway with the principal, she saw that every child they passed stopped to look at her, eyeing her from head to toe. When they entered the classroom, the principal spoke first with the teacher and then addressed the class. Klara heard her say "Claire" several times. But

KLARA AND CHANA

she had no idea what the principal was saying about her.

The principal left the class and the teacher led Claire to an empty desk at the back of the room.

Claire sat at that desk from February until June, understanding very little of what the teacher or anyone else said to her. Although her understanding came slowly, she attended class every day and paid as close attention to the teacher as she could.

Just like the students in the class stared at Claire, she paid attention to them. It didn't take but a couple of days for her to recognize that the new shoes Uncle Max had given her to wear looked like other children's shoes. But the hand-me-down clothes that she brought with her from Europe didn't look anything like what her classmates were wearing. In her third-grade class Claire didn't learn very much in the way of reading, writing and arithmetic, but her English vocabulary grew. And she learned a lot about how to be an American.

The Social Worker

Late one afternoon, Chana and Claire heard a knock on the door. A nicely dressed woman entered their little room and introduced herself as Miss Katz, a social worker from HIAS.

After taking down basic information she explained in Yiddish, "Do you know, Mrs. Bressler, that since you have a small child like your daughter, you can stay home and not have to go to work."

"Why should I do that?" retorted Chana. "How would we eat and pay the rent?" Chana felt the blood rise to her cheeks.

"HIAS will help. We will arrange the funds for you. Welfare of sorts. And you would be free to care for your child the way you would like," the lady explained, very pleased with her offer.

When Chana heard the word "welfare" her hands started to shake. Her anger elevated rapidly as she thought, *Did this young woman understand that I am Chana Koenig Bressler from Nadworna? That Koenigs and Bresslers were practically aristocracy before the accursed war? Did this snippet of a girl know how much tzedakah her family gave to the poor? Does she realize what I had to endure to survive the inferno of hell I've been through?*

"How dare you offer me charity! I have two strong hands." Chana held up her hands for Miss Katz to see. "I can support myself and my daughter. I don't need you or HIAS or your welfare!"

The young woman apologized to Chana, gathered her papers and stood up. She looked pityingly at Claire and glanced again at Chana before walking out of the door.

When Max found out that Chana had turned down the funds that HIAS had offered her, he couldn't understand why.

"Wouldn't you rather be home to take care of your daughter, than have to go out to work?" he asked Chana. During the war many women in America responded to the call to defend the country by taking jobs that allowed men to assume active military duty. But the prevailing role of women was to be at home to care for the children. Even though Anna did work with him daily in their store in the hours Barbara and Martin were in school, Max believed that Chana should be at home. He thought Klara needed more care from a loving mother.

In addition, Max wanted to support his sister as much as he could but there was a limit as to how long he'd be able to help her financially. The money from HIAS would have made things easier for Max. Tension mounted between Chana and her brother. She didn't like needing his money. The visits to Max and Anna's house became not so pleasant for Klara who didn't get any warmth and friendship from her cousins.

Chana's adjustment to America wasn't going smoothly. She could speak English to get by but wasn't fluent enough for a well-paying job. She had to take work at a clothing factory sewing piecework, which she hated. She had no satisfaction doing piecework. She couldn't use her skill and talent in sewing because she never had an entire garment to sew, only pieces. Paid by the piece, she worked long hours but earned very little. The airless factory was crowded and no one had a moment to be friendly to anyone else. Chana started to doubt if she would ever fit in to the American way of life.

A Change of Location

Hoping that a change of location would change her luck and brighten her up, Chana moved out of the Bronx to an apartment on Manhattan's Lower East Side on Avenue B between 12th and 13th Streets – 375 Avenue B Apt. 3F. She also hoped to relieve the tension with her brother that had built up in the six months of living across the street from Max and his family.

The apartment had three rooms. The kitchen had the bathtub in it and over the bathtub was a fitted metal top that also served as a table. Right in front of the bathtub was a huge window which looked onto Avenue B. Off the kitchen was the toilet with a long pull-down string. There was a bedroom where Chana slept and the third room was a small narrow storage room where Claire slept.

Claire was happy to move. She hadn't made any good friends at school and definitely wouldn't miss her cousins. And she understood English much better after her five months in third grade and now felt comfortable following the school routines. She knew that she needed to learn how to read and write English, but what she wanted most in the new school was a good friend. She hoped that she would find one in her new school.

Life for the ten-year-old was anything but easy at first. She still stood out as an immigrant. She couldn't hide her heavy accent and hadn't accumulated a large enough wardrobe so she wouldn't have to wear her hand-me-down old-fashioned clothes from Europe. The Jewish kids called her a 'greener' and laughed at her clothes and accent. They avoided her. The Christian kids teased her. One boy said to her, "Hey Hitler's wife – go back where you came from!" The only one that would play with her was Jenny, the only black girl in the class. No one wanted to be Jenny's friend, and Jenny couldn't understand why Claire wanted to be her friend.

Miss Smith, Claire's teacher, thought it would help Claire to sit with someone who was of Polish descent. So the teacher sat

Claire at the same table with Stella Schaplery, whose parents were Polish. But Stella was very cool to Claire at first. She didn't want to risk losing any of her friends by becoming too friendly with someone everyone else made fun of. But to herself, Stella thought Claire was a nice girl.

Miss Smith announced that every day children may buy a chocolate-covered graham cracker for a snack. Everyone was to bring two cents tomorrow to get a cracker. Claire had never seen a cookie completely covered in chocolate. But she also knew that she didn't have the two cents to buy one.

The next day before recess Miss Smith brought out the graham crackers and row by row the children came to the front of the class to buy their treat. When Claire's row was called, everyone lined up except Claire. She stayed in her seat. When Stella brought her graham cracker back to their table, Claire couldn't help but stare at the delicious treat. She tried to look away so as not to let Stella see how much she wanted it.

Stella said to Claire, "Did you forget your money? Here, have a piece of mine." Stella broke off a small piece of her graham cracker and handed it under the table to Claire so no one would see.

At home that night Claire thought about the chocolate treat Stella shared with her. She tasted the crunchy cracker and chocolate flavor. Claire wanted a whole chocolate-covered graham cracker in school like everyone else, but she had no money of her own and she dared not ask her mother for the two cents. She would certainly be refused.

The next day when recess began, Claire busied herself at her table as her classmates lined up to buy the graham cracker treat. She began writing her spelling words on a paper to make it look like she wasn't interested in the chocolate delight.

Chapter 8: America!

"Come with me, Claire; let's get our treat before only the broken pieces are left."

"That's okay, Stella. I'm not hungry now," Claire lied. She quickly looked down at her paper to avoid Stella's eyes.

When Stella returned to the table with her treat she asked Claire, "Don't you like chocolate? I love it. Yesterday you ate the piece I gave you. How come you didn't get a graham cracker today? Everyone gets one."

"I told you. I'm not hungry." And Claire continued to copy her spelling words. Within a few minutes everyone finished eating their snacks and left the room for outdoor recess. Claire stayed at her table. Only she and Miss Smith remained in the room.

Miss Smith walked up to Claire's table and gently asked, "Claire, why aren't you going out to recess? Do you feel alright?"

"I'm alright. I wanted to copy my spelling words," Claire answered.

Miss Smith said, "You will have time later to copy your words, Claire. Now it is recess and it's important to get some fresh air. But first, tell me, Claire. I see that you didn't come up for a graham cracker today. Do you like chocolate-covered graham crackers?"

"Yes, Miss Smith. Very much, but I forgot my money," Claire answered, and looked down at her paper.

"I see," said Miss Smith, knowingly.

Miss Smith put her hand on Claire's shoulder, smiled warmly at her and said, "Tomorrow, if you also forget your money, get in line anyway. I always have an extra graham cracker in case someone forgets their money." Every day until the end of the school year Miss Smith had an "extra" chocolate-covered graham cracker for Claire because every day she "forgot" her two cents.

Friends

Stella and Claire became friends. One day Stella invited Claire home with her after school. Claire was both excited and nervous about going to Stella's home. *Does her mother know I'm coming home with her? What if her mother doesn't like me and won't let me in?*

As the girls approached the house Claire asked Stella, "Does your mother always let you bring friends home with you after school?"

Stella smiled and said, "Yes, my mother likes to know who my friends are and have them come to our home to play with me."

Stella's mother greeted Claire warmly. She served the girls butter cookies and milk and asked Claire lots of questions about how she was getting along in school and what she thought about America. Claire felt so comfortable with Stella's mother who was taking such an interest in her. At the same time she was in disbelief that Stella's mother could be so soft and kind.

Stella led Claire to her bedroom. The first things Claire saw in the room were two dolls propped up on Stella's bed pillow.

Claire was wide-eyed and asked Stella, "How did you get these dolls?"

Stella laughed and answered, "My grandma and grandpa gave them to me for my birthday. I love the bride doll. Isn't her dress beautiful? One day I'm going to be a bride. Do you want to be a bride one day and have a beautiful white dress and tiara like my doll?"

Claire didn't know how to respond. She never had a real doll of her own and she never had grandparents to give her gifts. Her thoughts and feelings were whizzing through her mind.

Suddenly she felt pain again in her stomach. All she could see were the potato dolls she was playing with when the Nazis invaded her village. She tried to shut down the images of the past that invaded her mind but she couldn't. Her stomach hurt her too much to stay in the room with Stella and her two dolls.

Abruptly she said, "I have to go now. My mother needs me at home. Maybe I can come again another time."

Chapter 9
A Working Girl

Claire didn't like spending afternoons by herself in their small apartment waiting for her mother to come home from work. So she got herself a job at a children's clothing store on the street where they lived. She boldly walked into the store and asked the owner for a job.

She confidently said to him, "I am a very good cleaner. I will come every day after school and sweep out your store."

He said, "You're hired. Twenty-five cents a day. Be here exactly on time. But listen to me very carefully. You must do what I'm going to tell you now. The bell above the door rings when the door opens. When you hear the bell ring, drop the broom and run like the wind to the back of the store. Hide behind the supply closet! And stay there until I tell you to come out. If the city inspectors catch you working here I might be fined and maybe even put in jail for employing under-aged workers."

Claire agreed on the spot and asked the owner, "OK. Where's the broom?"

Each day as soon as she arrived at the store she went straight to the supply closet in the back. She took the broom and dust pan and methodically swept up and down each aisle where the customers walked. Nobody told her to, but she even swept under the shelves and racks. Claire prided herself on being a very good cleaner, never missing even a speck of dust. She didn't like having to hide every time the bell tingled and didn't really understand why she had to, but she liked to work so she followed directions. She also liked how it felt walking home with twenty-five cents in her pocket.

When she got home from work she handed the twenty-five cents to her mother. Claire was not allowed to keep any of the money for herself. Her mother told her that the money was needed to pay for her food and rent. That there was not enough left over for Claire to spend.

Claire had assigned jobs to do at home. She prepared breakfast every morning for her mother and herself. She made the sandwiches for their lunch. She was to have supper ready on the table when Chana came home. And she was responsible for cleaning the house. Claire was truly a good worker. After supper, Chana went out to night school to learn English, leaving Claire at home alone. Most nights Claire didn't see her mother until breakfast the next morning.

Sundays at the Movies

Only on Sundays did mother and daughter spend any time together. They took the subway uptown to the Bronx to visit Uncle Max and Aunt Anna and cousins Martin and Barbara. Claire waited all week for the Sunday outing. The subways were an adventure. It amazed her that there was "life" underground with people running from train to train. She loved sitting in the train looking at all the people. Until she came to America she had never seen dark-skinned or Asian people. She studied the clothes people wore. She listened closely when she could to the languages people spoke. She even liked the rumble and screeching of the trains; it was a kind of music to Claire. It was a long, stuffy, bouncy ride from the Lower East Side to the Bronx but she felt she was exploring America.

Cousin Martin always met them at the subway station. Following strict instructions from his father to be nice to his cousin, Martin kissed Claire on the cheek. Claire didn't like Martin or his kiss but she accepted it, thinking that it was an American thing to do in families. Martin then took them to his house where the whole family sat together for a large meal. Claire loved Uncle Max and Aunt Anna. They were warm and generous toward her. With them she felt like she had a family. Being with her mother wasn't like being in a family. They were more like two people who happened to live in the same small apartment; but it didn't feel anything like being with her Bronx family.

Very often after the meal Martin took Claire to a matinee at the local movie house. Claire could tell that he was not happy about his assignment and that he didn't like her very much. But going to the movies made it worthwhile for Claire to put up with her cousin's unfriendly behavior. The comedy routines of Abbott and Costello and Dean Martin - Jerry Lewis were her favorite movies. Mostly, she couldn't follow the fast dialogue, but that didn't matter. The slapstick antics made her laugh. And laughing, real belly-laughing, was a new experience. There had not been anything to laugh about in her life before the movies.

But the movies ended and Sunday became Monday, and the routines in Claire's life started over again.

Chapter 9: A Working Girl

The move to the Lower East Side was not working out for Chana or Claire. Chana felt trapped in her piece-work factory job. It didn't pay much and the long hours left her exhausted. Coming from work in the evening and then going to night school to improve her English left her with no time to herself. America was not the *Goldene Medina* for Chana. Chana's mood darkened. To Claire she complained about work, repeatedly voicing the pain she felt losing her parents and her husband, and vividly recounting the horrors in her life she had witnessed. The one day of brightness in the week stopped being fun. They would leave the Bronx and Chana would bemoan the fact that she didn't have a nice home of her own with dark-wood furniture and china dishes like she had before the war. Abruptly, the Sunday outings to Max and Anna stopped.

And so did laughing in the movies Claire didn't know where to turn. She was not happy in school. Her progress in learning to read and write English was slow. And she wasn't getting the hang of arithmetic. But mostly, she wasn't making friends. Her classmates were still not accepting her. She went to school because she had to, but she didn't like it.

Flash Cards

Claire had another job for a few short months. She tutored a young boy in arithmetic. Claire never went to first and second grade and wasn't up to grade level in mathematics, but she could handle simple arithmetic. She sat with the boy at the dining-room table in his house and tried valiantly to interest him.

"Come on, Joey, let's practice addition and subtraction. What if you have six cookies," cajoled Claire, "and you give two to...."

"I don't want to learn numbers," pouted Joey. "I want to play cards. You want to play rummy with me?"

"We'll play after we learn your homework. I promise."

"No. I want to play cards." Joey ran out of the room and got a deck of cards.

Claire didn't know what to do. Finally, a light went on in her head. "Okay," Claire said agreeably, "Let's play cards."

Joey dealt seven cards to Claire and seven to himself.

"Joey, if you have seven cards and pick two more from the pile, how many do you have?"

"Nine. I have nine."

"And if you give me five cards, how many do you have left?"

"I have four. An ace, two 7's and a 3 of clubs."

"Okay. And if you put the 7 and 3 together, how many is that?"

"That's 10!"

"Hey, Joey, you really know your numbers!"

Joey grinned. Claire continued this way every tutoring session, teaching addition and subtraction while they played rummy. For her work, she received the unheard of sum (in 1951) of 5 dollars an hour. That money also went to her mother to help pay the rent.

The Home

At age eleven the ever-present pains in her stomach were diagnosed as ulcers. The doctor said, "Stress is the cause." She was put on a special diet and given pills to quell the pain, but nothing seemed to work.

Chapter 9: A Working Girl

One morning, Chana said to Claire, "Pack your things. You're going to live somewhere else."

"Where are we moving to, Mama?" Claire asked.

"I'm not moving anywhere, but I found a place for you. You'll be in a place with other girls your age."

Claire was startled by her mother's answer. "I'm going to move without Mama? I'm going to live with strangers?" These thoughts troubled Claire. She did want to move somewhere else; to a nicer apartment in a friendlier neighborhood where she'd meet nicer children in school. But still. After thinking about it, maybe it would be better than the life she had now.

The place Chana wanted to send Claire to was a home for troublesome girls. Chana and Claire went there to meet the man in charge. He asked Chana all kinds of questions about Claire and her behavior and habits. Then Chana filled out many papers and gave them to the man.

Scanning the papers quickly, he said, "Everything seems to be in order. That will be $10 a month."

"What?" Chana answered in disbelief.

"Yes. $10 a month for room and board and other necessities."

Chana didn't know what to do. "I can't pay $10 a month."

"I'm sorry," he intoned, "then we can't take her."

Claire was heartbroken. Her hopes for a different, more peaceful life were dashed. Chana went silent. The two returned to their apartment on the Lower East Side without exchanging a single word.

Runaway

Claire wanted to get away from the despair and worry of her mother and the frustration from failure at school. She decided to run away. She couldn't run to Uncle Max and Aunt Anna because they would just make her go back home to her mother. Besides, Martin and Barbara hated Claire. There was only one other place she could go – to her Aunt Giza in Norfolk, Virginia. Aunt Giza had immigrated with her husband Sam Horowitz under Max's sponsorship not long after Chana and Claire.

Claire remembered Aunt Giza from Ansbach. Aunt Giza was pretty and walked with her head held high, full of self-confidence. Claire knew her aunt as warm and loving and never talking about the war. In every letter that Chana wrote to her sister, Claire added her own message of love and attachment. Claire's mind was made up. She would go to Aunt Giza in Norfolk, Virginia as soon as possible.

At school the next day, Claire asked her teacher where Norfolk, Virginia is. The teacher took out a map of the United States and said, "Here's where we are now, in New York City. To get to Norfolk, Virginia you have to go south in a car or on the train. It's a long way from New York. How come you are asking about Norfolk, Virginia? Do you know someone there, Claire?"

"My Aunt Giza lives there," Claire answered.

At recess she went outside and looked around the school yard. She silently addressed the playground. "Goodbye, nasty children. I'm glad I won't see you anymore."

That night when Chana was at night school, Claire packed her small suitcase with her favorite American-style dress, the new shoes that Uncle Max had given her to start the school year, and her stomach pills. As she lay in bed her thoughts raced. *Will I find*

Chapter 9: A Working Girl

a train to Norfolk, Virginia? How surprised the children at school will be when they hear. Will Uncle Max and Aunt Anna be upset? Martin and Barbara won't be. I hope Mr. Levy finds someone else to sweep his store. And how good it will be with Aunt Giza; she will take care of me. When Claire heard her mother come in she pretended to be asleep. Claire thought, *What will mother do when she finds me gone? Will she be angry and come to Aunt Giza's to get me? Or maybe she'll be happy that she doesn't have to take care of me any more and let me stay there?* Claire hardly slept, anxiously awaiting the morning.

As soon as Chana left for work in the morning, Claire quickly made peanut butter and jelly sandwiches to take with her. She packed an orange and the sandwiches in a little bag which she put in her suitcase. She was ready to go. Without hesitation or emotion she looked around the apartment and said, "Goodbye, Mama," and walked out.

Claire took it step by step. She walked down the stairway to the subway to Grand Central Station. When the man in the token booth wasn't looking she slipped under the turnstile and ran to the end of the platform. At Grand Central she approached a policeman and asked him where to find the train to Norfolk, Virginia. He pointed to a kiosk in the middle of the large room and told her to ask there.

At the kiosk Claire got in line behind several people. She practiced saying to herself "Where will I find the train to Norfolk, Virginia?" When she got to the counter she had to stand on her tiptoes to see the lady in the ticket booth. She was well-prepared with her question and the lady answered, "Gate 3, platform 6, leaving at 9 a.m. sharp. Round trip or one-way?"

Claire repeated, "Gate 3, platform 6, leaving at 9 a.m. sharp. Round trip or one-way."

The ticket lady said, "Round trip or one-way? Which is it?"

Claire didn't understand what the lady meant by "round trip or one-way," so she said "thank you" and left the kiosk.

Claire looked at the big clock on the wall and saw that she had about one hour before the train left. She went back to the policeman she first met and asked him where Gate 3, platform 6 was. He pointed to the far side of the large room and said, "See that big number 3 on the wall. That's Gate 3. Inside there you'll find platform 6. Where are you going?"

"To my Aunt Giza in Norfolk, Virginia," Claire confidently replied.

"You're pretty small to be going to Norfolk, Virginia by yourself. Somebody with you?" he asked.

Claire nodded, turned and walked quickly to where the policeman pointed. Inside the gate she saw trains lined up at the many platforms and people getting on and off. She saw number 6 above the last platform and walked to it. A train was standing there but there weren't very many people getting on it. She found a bench on the platform next to the train, put her suitcase down beside her and waited. A man wobbled down the platform and sat down on the far end of the bench. He loudly said to her, "This train going to Norfolk at 9 a.m. sharp?"

She answered, "Yes," feeling very proud of herself that everything was working out as she planned. The man looked at his watch, took a small bottle out of his jacket, swigged twice, leaned back, closed his eyes and began to snore. Claire got up and walked away.

She paid close attention to who was getting on the train. She eyed a family with several children coming onto the platform. As they boarded the train she too boarded, keeping a short distance behind them. After the parents found seats for themselves, the children spread out so they could all sit by a window. Three of the children sat at the window across the aisle from their parents. Claire sat in the window seat in the row directly behind the three children. Two other children sat directly behind their parents across the aisle from Claire. She put her suitcase on the seat next to her, hoping no one would sit there.

The train pulled out of the station and Claire was both excited and nervous. She was on her way to Aunt Giza, but she had no ticket and no money to buy one. She hoped she'd be able to dodge the conductor when he came to collect the tickets. When the conductor entered the car, the children from the family were bouncing on their seats and shouting about everything they saw out the window. Claire sat on her knees and looked out her window. She motioned to the children next to her and asked them what they saw. She wanted it to look like she was one of their family. It worked. The conductor punched the tickets from the parents and moved down the aisle. He never even looked up at the children or Claire. Relieved and emboldened, she sat down in her chair and enjoyed the ride.

She took out the orange and thought of Shnappsie and sailing across the Atlantic. She recalled the train ride from Boston with Uncle Max and how he laughed when she asked him, "Where is the gold, Uncle Max?" She remembered him saying that you have to work hard in America to find the gold. Claire had certainly seen how true it was. There wasn't any gold on the streets in the *Goldene Medina*. That was for sure! The changing scenes of countryside, town and city fascinated Claire. She loved adventure and she was now on a big one. By herself in America, going to be with her Aunt Giza who she knew would take care of her.

When the train arrived in Norfolk, it was late afternoon. Claire knew she had to take a ferry to Aunt Giza's house. Aunt Giza had written about the ferry ride several times in her letters. In the train station she showed the paper with Aunt Giza's address to a policeman and asked him how to get to the ferry that would take her there. He said, "You can walk through Harbor Park. It will take you about twenty-five minutes if you walk fast. Want me to show you?" He led Claire out of the train station and said, "Follow this pathway and don't go off it, and you'll get right to the ferry. You walking by yourself, little girl? I don't know about that." Claire just said "Thank you," and ran down the pathway.

She used the same trick at the ferry she had used on the train. She attached herself to a family with children and walked onto the ferry right alongside them. Once the ferry started to move she went to the rail to see what she could see. *I hope I don't get sick on this ride,* she said to herself. Claire breathed deeply to take in the salt air. The ride was smooth and she felt calm. *Does anyone miss me?* she wondered. *I don't care. I'm going to see Aunt Giza. I know she will take care of me.*

When the ferry docked, Claire showed Aunt Giza's address to someone who pointed her in the right direction. As she walked, she showed the paper to whomever she could and asked if this was the way to Aunt Giza.

When Claire arrived at the address on the paper it was dark. She stood for several moments on the sidewalk in front of the house and thought, "This morning I was in my apartment in New York City and now I'm in front of Aunt Giza's house in Norfolk, Virginia. I did it. All by myself. I'm free now." With a giant smile on her face Claire knocked on the door. Giza called through the door, "Who is it?"

Claire said, "It's me, Aunt Giza." Giza opened the door and gasped when she saw her little niece standing there. She reached down and hugged Claire tightly.

"Klartchu, sweet girl. What are you doing here? Is everything alright? Where's your mother? Are you alone? She didn't write and tell me that you were coming. How did you get here? Come in, Klartchu, come in."

Giza took Claire's suitcase and put it down by the door. She took Claire's hand and led her into the kitchen. "Sit down, Klartchu. You've had a long day," Giza said.

For the first time since she walked out of her home that morning, Claire let her guard down. She was with her Aunt Giza. She was safe. She sat down, her shoulders dropped, she sighed deeply, and tears began to flow. Gently at first, but then more intensely until she was heaving deep sobs. Catching her breath, Claire was able to say through her tears, "I can't. I can't take it anymore."

Giza wrapped the child in her warm and loving arms and held on to her till her sobbing subsided.

"I know. I know. You have been through so much, my sweet Klartchu. But your mother will be so worried. We must tell her you are here," Giza said. Wanting to calm and reassure Claire, her aunt took hot water from a samovar on the table and made tea. She mixed in honey and lemon juice and placed it in front of Claire.

"Drink this, Klartchu. It will warm you up. Let me get you a cinnamon bun. I baked it this afternoon. I'm sure you're hungry."

Claire was hungry and exhausted, but she didn't touch either food or drink. Instead she pleaded, "No, Aunt Giza. Please don't tell Mama. Promise me that you won't say anything."

Giza saw the pain in Claire's eyes and responded, "You are here now with me, Klartchu. I will take care of you. You need to rest from your long journey. That was quite a trip to take all by yourself. You have grown up a lot, Klartchu. You aren't the little Klartchu any more that I knew in Ansbach. Come, I will show you your room and the bath. Tomorrow we will talk more."

Giza understood how difficult it must be for the child to be with Chana. Giza knew that her sister suffered deeply from the loss of her husband, their parents, and the respected comfortable life she once had. In the letters they exchanged, Giza heard the bitterness and despair that engulfed Chana. *How fortunate I am,* thought Giza. *I have a husband who has good work which supports us. We have a new baby. We are living in a nice neighborhood in our own home. It is so hard for Chana. She has to do piece work in a factory that hardly gives her enough to live on, let alone properly raise Klartchu. Poor girl,* Giza thought about her niece; *that she is growing up with a mother so troubled by her past and so challenged in her present.*

Giza knew that she must care for Claire now, but how could she not tell Chana, adding yet more pain to her sister's life? She didn't know what to do.

Giza took Claire to the guest room.

"This will be your room, Klartchu. The bathroom is right next to your room. Uncle Sam's and my room is at the end of the hall. The room between us is for Frieda, your cousin. She's just a baby but you'll love her. She is so adorable. She'll love you, too. You'll meet her tomorrow. Now, wash up and go to sleep. Everything will be okay, Klartchu. I am so happy to see you. Do you want anything now?" Giza asked.

"May I have the cinnamon bun you made, please?"

"Of course, and I'll make you a new tea that is hot. I'll be back

Chapter 9: A Working Girl

in a minute."

Claire sat on the bed and took off her shoes. She lay back and sank in the soft quilt. It felt so comfortable after all the stress of traveling. She closed her eyes.

When she opened her eyes again sunlight was lighting up her room. She heard birds chirping outside her window. She sat up and saw the cinnamon bun and tea on the night table next to her bed. She heard a knock at the door and a baby crying.

"Good morning, Klartchu," Aunt Giza called through the slightly open door. "Cousin Frieda wants to meet you. May we come in?"

Giza walked in, holding a pudgy baby swathed in pink. "This is Frieda. She's nine months old. She was named after your saintly grandmother Frieda, my and your mama's mother. Do you want to hold her, Klartchu?" and handed the baby to Claire.

Claire cradled Frieda in the crook of her arm the way she had seen mamas do with their babies.

"That's so good how you are holding her," Giza said. "Look how Frieda is looking right at you. She likes you, Klartchu. She feels safe with you."

Claire smiled. She thought, I like holding Frieda. I will be a good mama one day.

"Can I give her a bottle, Aunt Giza?"

"Not now, Klartchu. I just fed her. Let's give you some food. You haven't eaten for almost a whole day. You didn't even eat the cinnamon bun." Giza prepared a hot meal for Claire which she devoured. After eating, Claire played with Frieda on the floor in the living room.

After a time Giza said to Claire, "Can you smell that Frieda needs a diaper change? Let me show you how to change her diaper." Giza showed Claire how to unpin each side of the cloth diaper, use it to wipe up as much as she could, gently wash off Frieda, and then dry, powder and pin the fresh diaper.

"The dirty diaper goes in the pail on the back porch. Make sure the cover is on the pail after you put in the diaper."

Two days after Claire arrived at Giza's, Chana called. She was frantically upset.

"Giza, I don't know where Klara is. She ran away. I went to the police and they don't know where she is. Her teacher told me Klara asked her where Norfolk is and said her aunt lives there. Is Klara with you? Tell me, Giza."

Giza answered, "Yes, Klara is here, and she is okay."

"Why didn't you call me, Giza? How long were you going to let me suffer before telling me?" Chana screamed over the phone.

"I was waiting for you to call, Chana. I waited because I needed to know if you want Klara to come back. It has been very hard for you since coming to America, I know. And maybe it would help you to not have to watch out for Klara for a while. To just take care of yourself. I also know that Klara is a willful little girl whose life has been disrupted many times. And she can be hard to handle. She came here, Chana, looking for a safe, loving place to be. Klara came here because she felt she had to get away from everything in her life in New York. If you want her to come back I will send her back. But not right now. Let her stay here for another couple of weeks. She needs a rest. And so do you, Chana."

"I'm angry with you that you didn't call me, Giza. I do need a rest, but I want Klara to come back. I'm her mother and she needs to be with me."

The next day, as Claire was changing Frieda's diaper, Giza said to Claire, "Klartchu, you are such a good little mama."

Claire smiled at the compliment. She said, "I can stay here with you and Frieda and Uncle Sam, and go to school here. And when I come home from school I'll take care of Frieda so you can rest, Aunt Giza."

"You would be a big help," Giza said. "But your mother would miss you so much. Let's just take it day by day."

Claire stayed with Aunt Giza for three blissful weeks, basking in Giza's care and love. Claire learned how to feed Frieda. Giza showed her how to bathe the baby. Claire sang to Frieda and gently bounced her on her knee.

At the end of three weeks, Giza explained to Klara, "We love having you here with us, Klartchu, but your mother called and she is sick with worry. She told me that you ran away and she doesn't know where to turn. I'm sorry sweetheart, but I had to tell your mother. I couldn't keep it from her any longer. My dear sweet girl, you have to go back now."

Claire was once again heartbroken, but after some time she relented. Aunt Giza gave her money for the boat and the train and then some. She packed her food for the journey and filled her with words of hope and encouragement. Claire reluctantly left her paradise to return to her mother and New York and school and all that it entailed.

Chapter 10
Returning Home

On the train ride home Claire sat alone on a seat next to the window. As the houses and farmlands and forests whizzed past her she felt sad and afraid.

I was so happy at Aunt Giza's house. I was free. Whenever Aunt Giza called me Klartchu I felt like I was part of a family. I had so much fun playing with baby Frieda. And I learned all about how to take care of babies. I loved that.

But I have nothing to look forward to back home, Claire thought. *Aunt Giza said Mama was upset and worried. What is Mama going to do to me because I ran away and didn't call to tell her that I was at Aunt Giza's?*

And I hate school. My teacher is okay, but I have no friends there.

I'm going to be alone in the apartment, cleaning and cooking and whatever else Mama tells me to do.

Claire felt she had nothing to look forward to, being back home.

Chapter 10: Returning Home

When she arrived at Grand Central Station, the last stop, Claire gathered her few belongings and stepped off the train. The big clock in the main entry area read 6:38 p.m.

Arriving home, she entered a cold, dark apartment. Claire felt relieved that she didn't have to see her mother right now. Her mother wouldn't be home from work for at least another three hours. Claire was too tired and upset to have to explain herself.

Claire was more tired than hungry, so she hung up her clothes, hid the money Aunt Giza had given her, washed up, went to bed and immediately fell asleep.

The key turning in the front-door lock woke Claire up. She rolled onto her left side and looked at the clock on the nightstand. 10:10 p.m. As Chana entered the bedroom Claire sat up.

"You're back," Chana said to Claire. "I'm exhausted. There's a loaf of bread in the breadbox. Make me an extra sandwich in the morning as I'll be staying late again tomorrow night. And make sure you get to school on time tomorrow. I've had enough dealing with your school with you running away." Chaya turned and walked into the bathroom. Claire made sure the alarm clock was set for 5:30 and lay down again. She turned her face to the wall and closed her eyes. She felt a heavy load in her heart and hoped sleep would take it away. But Claire lay staring at the wall until long after her mother had fallen asleep.

Claire walked into her class as the 9:00 a.m. bell rang.

"Welcome back, Claire," her teacher said. "We missed you. Take your same seat. And we'll start our lessons."

At recess Claire went out to the playground. A couple of her classmates came up to her and said, "We heard you ran away from home. Where'd you go?"

"I didn't run away from home. I went to visit my aunt in Norfolk, Virginia."

"Oh," they said, and walked away.

The school year continued without incident. Claire came to school, did whatever she could when she understood what to do, and mostly spent recess by herself.

Nothing changed at home. All of Claire's responsibilities continued. As did her loneliness.

She wrote letters to Aunt Giza asking if she could come back and live with her. The response was always the same–*not now, Klartchu.*

In the fall she would start junior high school located in a different neighborhood. Maybe she'd make a friend there, she hoped.

Gloria

Junior high school was different. Instead of having one teacher and sitting in the same room all day, Claire went from one classroom to another and each class had a different teacher. Walking through the school she saw lots of kids, but there wasn't much opportunity to meet anyone. Everyone seemed to be in motion all the time. And at lunch time, the same kids sat together in groups, and didn't talk with any other groups. Claire once again felt she didn't have a place in junior high school.

After school one day, Claire was walking home alone. About three blocks away from school she heard a voice calling her name. She turned around to see a pack of boys running toward her. Again, the voice called her and it didn't sound friendly. Sensing danger, Claire started to run. She had no idea why anyone would be after her, but she was smart enough to know it was better not to find out. She got to the corner and remembered seeing mothers with their young children in the park just down the street to her left. She thought no one would dare try to hurt her if there were other people around.

She ran into the park but it was empty. She didn't chance running out again because if the boys were after her they'd surely catch her at the entrance. She saw a small grove of trees behind the swings at the far edge of the park. She sprinted with all her force toward the trees. The trees were thick with branches and leaves. She eyed a tree with a low-lying branch. She threw her book bag into a clump of bushes and pulled herself onto the branch. Her heart was pounding wildly as she climbed higher into the tree, hoping she couldn't be seen.

In less than a minute seven or eight boys about her age charged into the park. One of them yelled, "Claire, we're gonna get you. We know you're here." Since the trees were the only place to hide in the park the pack ran toward them. Claire froze, holding her breath so as not to move a leaf.

"Here's her bookbag," one particularly rough-looking boy yelled. He opened it up and dumped Claire's books on the ground. He took the pencils out of the bag and broke them in two.

"I found her," another boy screamed in triumph. "She's up in this tree."

The pack of boys surrounded the tree and began chanting, "We've got you, Claire. You're finished, Claire."

Claire had no clue why this was happening to her, but she knew she was trapped.

Two boys climbed onto the low branch and quickly reached

Claire. Each one grabbed a leg and began to pull her down. She had no choice but to climb down. She didn't want to fall out of the tree.

On the ground the rough-looking boy who found her book bag pushed her down so her back was against the tree.

Another unsavory looking kid took a stick and started to poke Claire with it.

Suddenly the mean faces of the vicious Polish brothers, Pawel and Lukasz, and their pack of nasty boys who beat her up beneath her cherry trees when she was five, flashed before her eyes. *I didn't cry then,* she thought, *and I won't cry now.*

Then all the boys started punching and kicking her.

She couldn't physically defend herself against this mob but she wasn't defeated. Claire looked up from the ground where she lay, held her head straight and shouted at them,

"Stop hitting me. I don't even know you. And you don't know me. Why are you doing this to me?" Startled by the force of Claire's command, they stopped.

"Gloria told us to; that's why," the one with the stick obediently answered.

Her voice taking on authority and strength, Claire asked, "Who's Gloria?"

"Gloria Marchetti. She gives the orders," he replied.

"Where does Gloria live?" Claire demanded.

"On the other side of the school where the Italians live," the hooligan with the stick volunteered. Then he turned to the pack and commanded, "Out of here," and the young thugs ran out of the park.

Chapter 10: Returning Home

Claire got up, brushed herself off, collected her books and went home.

At home, Claire tended to her wounds, washed up and changed clothes.

She looked in the phone book and found the exact address for Marchetti on the street the ringleader told her.

Chana wasn't going to be home for several hours yet, so Claire went out to find Gloria. The address for Marchetti was a dilapidated building many blocks from where Claire lived. Claire scanned the broken mailboxes outside the building entrance to find the Marchetti apartment. Luckily it was on the ground floor.

Fearlessly, Claire approached the apartment and knocked loudly on the door. She immediately turned and hid herself in the stairwell from where she could see who answered.

A large tough-looking girl wearing a pink angora sweater and straight black skirt with hair piled high on her head came to the door. So, this was Gloria. Claire had seen her at lunch, always with a crowd of kids around her, and also after school hanging out near the bus stop with some tough-looking boys and girls, most of whom were smoking.

Claire stepped out of the darkness of the stairwell into the light coming from inside Gloria's apartment.

"Gloria, remember me?" said Claire.

"Yeah."

"I understand you gave the orders to beat me up."

"Yeah," Gloria admitted proudly.

"Why?"

"For one, you talk funny, and you're probably a Jew," stated

Gloria emphatically.

"You're right, Gloria, I don't talk like you and I am a Jew." And with that Claire punched Gloria squarely in the stomach.

Letting out a loud moan, Gloria doubled over. Claire grabbed the hair on Gloria's head with two hands and yanked Gloria to her feet. With all her force she then punched Gloria in the jaw. Again, Gloria crumbled at Claire's feet.

"And just like your mob did to me," Claire said, she kicked the moaning Gloria in her ribs.

"And here's for my pencils," Claire said, pulling the helpless girl's hairdo apart along with fistfuls of black hair.

Standing tall and confident, Claire looked Gloria straight in her eyes and said, "If any of your crowd touches me again, next time you won't get up from the floor. And that's a promise!"

The rest of junior high school no one ever touched Claire. Ever.

The Truant

Claire didn't like junior high school. She wasn't making friends. She had too many teachers, each one wanting something different from her. And the teachers had so many students that they didn't seem to have time to connect with Claire. The lessons moved too quickly and Claire had difficulty understanding them.

I have better things to do with my time than to listen to some lady drone on and on about past participles, whatever they are, Claire thought. *I'd rather stay home.*

She decided she would stay home. She knew that her mother would never give her permission to stay home, so she didn't ask.

As she did every morning, Claire packed her mother's lunch

Chapter 10: Returning Home

and her own, said goodbye and walked out the door. But she didn't go to school. Instead, she waited under the dark stairwell until she heard her mother leave the apartment and lock the door. Claire waited in the stairwell long enough to be sure Chana didn't return to get something she forgot, and then she slipped back into the house. Once inside, she felt relieved and exhilarated.

I'm free. No one to tell me what to do. I can do whatever I want.

She put her sandwich in the refrigerator. She said to herself, "Don't forget to eat it. You don't want Mama to find it and ask why I didn't eat it."

Then she boiled water for a cup of tea. She put a huge dollop of honey in the steaming cup. She sat at the kitchen table with her cup of hot sweet tea and leisurely thumbed through a fashion magazine her mother had brought home.

This is how to start a morning, she thought.

When she finished her tea, she cleaned up the breakfast dishes and put away any food left out. She usually did this when she came home from school. With that chore completed, Claire turned on the radio to a rock and roll station she had discovered. Chana didn't like the rock and roll music and didn't let Claire listen to it when Chana was home. With no one to stop her, Claire turned up the volume and started to dance. As she jerked and twirled to the music, she picked up the feather duster and dusted her way through the apartment.

She straightened the beds and the pillows on the couch. She made sure the plants her mother loved were watered sufficiently.

This is fun, not work. I could do this every day.

And for two weeks straight that is what she did every day. On the first day of the third week, as Claire was sipping her tea and daydreaming about all the fancy clothes people wore, there was a knock at the door. She froze in her chair and gently put down her cup so it wouldn't make a noise. Another knock. Claire held her breath, afraid whoever was at the door would know someone was inside. A third knock. And then she saw an envelope sliding into the apartment under the door.

That's strange, Claire thought. *Who slips envelopes under the door? Letters go in the mailbox.*

She waited fifteen minutes before tiptoeing to the door to look at the envelope, but still did not pick it up.

I'm going to leave it there. Maybe whoever put it there is still standing outside waiting to see if someone is home.

After an hour, assuming no one was outside, Claire picked up the envelope.

It was addressed to Chana Bressler, from John Fitzpatrick, Truant Officer, New York City Public Schools. Claire knew who John Fitzpatrick was. Every kid in school knew who the truant officer was. Claire had never seen John Fitzpatrick, but she knew she didn't want to and didn't want her mother to either.

Claire tore open the envelope and read:

> *To: Mrs. Chana Bressler*
> *From: John Fitzpatrick, Truant Officer, New York City Public Schools, District 3*
> *Your daughter, Claire, has not been in school for two straight weeks. Please contact her school to tell us if you know this and why she isn't in school.*
> *John Fitzpatrick*
>
> *Truant Officer, New York City Public Schools, District 3*

I don't want Chana Bressler to know that her daughter has not been in

Chapter 10: Returning Home

school for two straight weeks, Claire said out loud. She tore up the letter and buried it deep in the garbage pail.

A couple of mornings later Claire was making sandwiches as usual. Chana asked her, "How's school? I haven't heard you say anything about it for weeks?"

"It's okay," she answered. "Here's your sandwich. I've got to go. I don't want to be late."

Claire didn't hide in the stairwell that morning. She went quickly to school. She came into her classroom several minutes earlier than usual. Her first period teacher greeted her and told her to first report to the office because she had been absent so long.

Claire had never had to report to the office for anything and didn't know what to expect. When she entered the office, the secretary coldly told her to sit down and wait for the vice-principal to call her in.

Several other students were also sitting outside the vice-principal's office. She recognized one of them as one of the pack of punks who had beaten her up in the park.

She looked straight at him and asked, "What are you doing here?"

"Fitzpatrick caught me ditching school again," he answered.

"What's going to happen to you?" Claire quizzed him.

"I don't know. Last time the v.p. said he might send me to another school somewhere away from around here if I ditch again. I don't care. I hate this school. We used to have fun chasing after kids but Gloria doesn't even do that any more," he said.

The vice-principal's door opened and a girl walked out crying. From inside the office the vice-principal called out "Claire

Bressler."

Claire entered the office. Looking down at a paper on his desk the vice-principal said, "Close the door." Claire did and remained standing.

"Claire Bressler, 7th grade," the vice-principal read from the paper. He looked up at Claire and said, "You've been out of school for over two weeks straight. And your mother didn't contact the school after the truant officer put a letter under your door. Does she know that you haven't been in school?"

Claire stood with her shoulders slightly dropping and in a quiet voice, "Yes, sir, she does," she boldly lied. "Mama has been sick for the last two weeks and I had to stay home to take care of her. It's only Mama and me at home. She couldn't go to work and just stayed in bed. She's finally better now."

The vice-principal said, "Claire, it is very good that you are the kind of girl who will take care of her mother. But please let the office know if you have to stay home for a long time for any reason. After a student is out for two weeks, if we don't hear from the home we send Mr. Fitzpatrick, the truant officer, to check up on what's happening. Lots of kids think they can ditch school but they can't. That's all, Claire. Here is a note letting you back in school to give your first period teacher. And I hope your mother stays well."

Claire took the note and said, "Thank you, sir." And she walked out smiling.

Throughout the remainder of her time in junior high, whenever she felt she needed it, Claire took a "vacation" from school, but never longer than two weeks at a time.

Saying Thank You

Chapter 10: Returning Home

As Chana walked out the door to work one morning, she said to Claire, "On your way home from school this afternoon find a clean cardboard box. I want to send a package to Poland."

"Where will I find a box, Mama?"

"I don't know. Just find one. And use bleach today to scrub the bathroom sink."

"Yes, Mama, I will."

As Claire walked home from school she saw the garbage cans lined up at the curb.

Tomorrow's garbage pick-up day. Maybe I'll be lucky to find a carton for Mama. Who does she want to send a package to in Poland? Aunt Giza lives in Virginia. And Pepi's in Israel. Who else is there?

Around the corner from her building Claire saw some boxes sitting on top of garbage cans. She picked three, each one a different size, and brought them home.

"Good, Claire. This shoe box is the right size I need," Chana said when she came home.

"Who are you sending a package to, Mama?"

"The Klimeks."

Claire was startled to hear Chana say the Klimeks. Chana spoke about the war all the time, but never mentioned the Klimeks.

"I'm sending them a large bag of rice, a long-sleeve cotton blouse I don't wear anymore and a box of Band-Aids."

"Why are you sending the Klimeks these things, Mama?"

"Didn't they do something good for you a long time ago? Shouldn't you say 'thank you' when someone does something to help you?"

"You're right, Mama. I have a Hershey's chocolate bar and some gum that I can put in the box."

Chana wrapped the Band-Aids, gum and Hershey's bar in a sheet of newspaper and put them in the box. She rolled up the blouse and placed it carefully on the side. She then opened up the bag of rice, slipped in it a 10-dollar bill and resealed the bag with scotch tape.

"Ten dollars is a lot of money, Mama. That's a big thank you."

Chana put the rice in the box and filled up the empty spaces with crumpled pieces of newspaper. She cut up a brown paper shopping bag from the A&P and wrapped the box in it. And then wrote the Klimeks' address on it.

"Tomorrow after school, take this box to the post office and ask them how much it will cost to send it and how long it will take to get there. Then bring it back home. I'll give you the exact money you need and you'll take it back to the post office to mail."

"Sure, Mama. I like the idea to say 'thank you' by sending a box of things. Let's do it again some time. We can send surprises to the Klimeks."

"Yes," Chana said, "they will be surprised."

Terror

The last years of junior high school were uneventful for Claire. Which wasn't so wonderful. Her social life didn't improve at all. Studies in school were not any easier or more interesting.

In her letters to Aunt Giza she begged to come live with her but she knew, of course, Chana would never approve. Claire missed baby Frieda's giggles and smiles so much. She longed for the satisfaction of caring for someone who needed her.

Chapter 10: Returning Home

Claire spent a lot of time alone at home. And when she did venture outside the house on one of her "vacation" days, she was constantly looking over her shoulder for Mr. Fitzpatrick who was vigilantly on patrol to catch truants.

She kept her eyes and ears open for a steady job she could do after school, but never found one. Day after day, there was not much happiness in Claire's life. Chana was out early each day and came back home late. They didn't go out anywhere. A few times Claire went by herself to the movies in the late afternoon, but she didn't have enough money to go as often as she would have liked.

With less than a month until the end of the school year, as usual Claire was walking home by herself after school. She had never been threatened by anyone in the neighborhood after she punched out Gloria, but she had heard reports of muggings and worse. With Chana often complaining that she didn't feel safe walking alone at night coming home from work, Claire was always alert to the activity on the street.

As Claire approached her street she heard screaming. She turned the corner and saw a woman leaning out of an apartment window on the third floor, looking down the street toward Claire's building and shrieking, "Anna's been murdered; Anna's dead." Down the block close to her building Claire saw police cars with their lights flashing and a crowd of people standing on the sidewalk.

Claire felt her heart pounding. *Mama,* she thought. People in the neighborhood often called her mama Anna, the English equivalent of Chana.

"Mama," Claire screamed in fright.

The blood rushed from Claire's head. She began to sweat. She ran down the block, crying "Mama, Mama." When she came up to the crowd she cried from the deepest place in her being, "Mama," and the crowd turned toward her and parted. Claire was stopped by a policeman standing in front of the crowd who kept her from advancing any closer to the crime scene.

"It's my mama," Claire screamed at the policeman.

The policeman gripped Claire's arm to hold her back and called to another policeman standing next to a patrol car, "The kid says it's her mama."

The officer by the car spoke back in his megaphone, "No, it isn't. The victim had no kids. Tell her to go home. It's not her mama."

The policeman holding Claire said to her, "Go home, kid. It's not your mama."

That night, when Chana came home Claire told her about what happened.

Chana responded, "Maybe it's time to move."

A New Start

In the summer before the start of Claire's first year in high school, Chana and Claire moved back to the Bronx. They rented an apartment at 175 Henwood Place in the southwest Bronx. It was definitely not a high-rent neighborhood, but it was a quiet street with buildings that were decently maintained. Chana believed they would be safe there.

Claire enrolled in William Howard Taft High School. In the early 1950s Taft had a relatively homogeneous student population. It drew from neighborhoods that were populated predominantly by Italian, Irish and Eastern European families.

Chapter 10: Returning Home

Once again Claire came into a new school where she knew no one. Even though Claire no longer had a Polish accent and sounded like she grew up in New York, making friends continued to be difficult. Outsiders breaking into high-school cliques didn't happen easily for anyone.

Claire was careful in her first few months at Taft to be on time to every class and to have a note from Chana if for some reason she was absent. She didn't want to be thought of as irresponsible or delinquent in any way. But she soon noticed that classmates would be out a day or two and return to class without any kind of excuse. Teachers didn't seem to be concerned or even aware that a student was absent. Claire took this observation to mean she could skip school and no one would notice. She tried it a couple of times and concluded she was right – teachers didn't seem to care if you were in class or not, as long as you weren't a trouble-maker. For the first two years at Taft, Claire took a lot of self-proclaimed "vacation" days.

On most days when she took off from school Claire stayed home. When she was certain that Chana was on her way to work and wouldn't be returning until evening, the first thing she did was turn on the radio to her favorite rock and roll station. She turned up the volume and no matter what song played, she danced. Dancing was as automatic to Claire as walking, but it was only when she was alone that she could sway and bounce and twirl to her soul's content. As she swept she danced. As she cooked she danced. When she took a break from her chores and sat at the table with a magazine, her feet continued to move to the beat of the music.

I just can't help myself, she thought. *My feet have a mind of their own.*

When she ventured out of the house, she didn't go much

beyond the big A&P supermarket several blocks away. While she didn't know if there were truant officers at Taft she didn't want to take any chances. If she met one, she could always say she was shopping for her mama who couldn't get out. It was true, she told herself, *Mama's at work and gets home late.*

Maggie O'Brien

On one of her "vacation" days, Claire danced downstairs to the lobby on her way to the A&P. When she got to the landing before reaching the bottom, she saw the superintendent of the building sweeping the hallways. Claire stopped and watched. The super was a young woman but she was all bent over as she swept. Claire had never seen a woman so young with a hunchback. The woman pushed a pile of dust and dirt into the dustpan and stopped. She straightened up as much as she could but still couldn't stand up straight. It didn't look to Claire like a comfortable or efficient way to sweep. The woman looked up and saw Claire standing on the landing. The super smiled and said, "Hello, you're new in the building aren't you? You're Chana's daughter, right? What's your name?"

"Claire."

"Hello, Claire. I'm Margaret Mary O'Brien. Call me Maggie. I'm the super and I live with my husband and three children in the corner apartment, 1-A, behind the stairwell. How do you like living here at 175 Henwood Place? I do my best to keep things tidy and running smoothly."

"I like it a lot. The building is clean and all the mailboxes have locks on them and it's pretty quiet most of the time. Do you do all the work around here?" Claire asked.

"I do the cleaning and some of the small repair jobs. I'd do more if I didn't have the three kids and if I didn't get so tired so quickly. I've got this problem with my back and I can't stand up straight. After standing or sitting for a long time, it starts to hurt me," Maggie said.

Claire said to herself, *Maybe I can help her with her children.*

Claire said to her, "I have to go to the A&P now but when I get back can I sweep up for you? Or throw away all the papers and junk that collect here? I'd be happy to help you."

"Thanks, Claire," she answered. "You are a sweet girl for offering. I'm okay doing this bit of work in the hallway. But I could use some help in my apartment. When you come back, knock on my door and we'll talk."

"Okay," Claire answered. "I won't be long. Bye." And Claire bopped out of the building, thinking *Maggie is nice; she has a friendly smile; I like her.*

On her return she knocked on apartment 1-A. No one answered so she knocked again. *Maybe she's resting. I'll try again later.* As Claire turned to leave she heard Maggie calling from inside, "If that's you, Claire, I'll be there in a minute."

Claire turned around and in a few moments the door opened. Maggie was standing bent over and holding an infant. "I was lying on the couch with the baby, trying to get a bit of rest. Come in. Put your grocery bag down by the door and sit at the table."

Claire walked in and looked around. The apartment wasn't neat and tidy like the lobby. Breakfast dishes were still in the sink, three clothes hampers were overflowing and toys were scattered across the floor. *Maggie does need help,* Claire said to herself. She sat down at the table.

Maggie said, "Here, hold Timothy. I'll get us something to drink. Will you join me for a beer?"

Beer? Claire thought. *Maggie drinks beer? At 10:30 in the morning?*

"No thank you," Claire answered.

"How about a root beer? Timothy loves root beer. I just give him a spoonful, but he laps it up," Maggie said.

"Okay, I like root beer," Claire answered, as she tickled Timothy's double chin. "He's cute. How old is he?"

"He's eleven months. He's big, isn't he? And heavy!" Maggie handed Claire a cold bottle of Dad's Old Fashioned Root Beer with two straws in it. In her other hand was a bottle of Pabst Blue Ribbon. Sitting on the table was a ceramic mug decorated with green shamrocks and a sly-looking leprechaun.

Maggie said, "This is my everyday mug. On the mantle in the living room I've got a fancy one that I use on special occasions. It belonged to my granddaddy, Shaun Fitzgerald, my mom's daddy. He loved his beer. I was his favorite grandchild and he left me his favorite mug in his will. From the time I was a wee one he would give me a sip of his beer from it when my mom wasn't looking. I'll show it to you later."

Maggie asked Claire, "Do you know how to pour a bottle of beer so it isn't all foamy? I'll show you." Maggie popped open the beer bottle and handed it and the mug to Claire.

"Hold the mug in one hand and tilt it slightly. Now pour in the beer but do it slowly. I like a little bit of foam but not a lot."

Claire followed Maggie's instructions and Maggie said, "Excellent, Claire. You're a fast learner. I'm gonna let you pour my beer all the time."

Claire wasn't sure why Maggie wanted her to pour the beer, but she said to herself, *If that helps Maggie and makes her happy, I'll do it any time she wants.*

Maggie took her mug and raised it in the air and said, "Today is my lucky day, Claire. You're a gift from heaven! Here's to you, Claire, a kindly soul, who has offered to help me. And oh my lord how I need help."

Claire picked up her bottle of root beer and without skipping a beat, Maggie clicked her mug to the bottle. Maggie put her mouth to her mug and threw back a huge gulp. A small white foam mustache lined Maggie's upper lip which she quickly wiped off with her tongue.

"Ah, a cold beer in the morning. It does the soul good and makes the work easier," Maggie chimed, and downed another gulp. "How's the root beer?"

"Really cold. Thank you."

"I most certainly can use your help, Claire. I can get my husband and the two older ones out in the morning and tidy up the lobby. But by then I'm knocked out and have to rest. Timothy's a handful, especially because he's so heavy. Look around, you can see what I can't seem to keep up with. If you can help me, especially in the afternoon when Conor and Erin are home, that would be the best. I'll pay you. Are you available in the afternoon?" Maggie asked in an almost pleading way.

"I'm available every day after school from 3 o'clock. What can I do?" Claire asked.

"Oh, bless you, Claire," Maggie said, downing another swig from her mug.

"Are you a careful dishwasher? My husband wants the dishes to sparkle. And washing the clothes. Do you know to separate the hot water and cold water items? I can't afford to shrink any more of my husband's shorts. Mostly, though, I need help with Conor and Erin. They are a handful, especially Conor. He can get wild and he's got a temper like his father. Erin is quiet but she can get into trouble. And picking up after the two of them – my back can't take much bending over."

"How does $1.25 an hour sound to you for your pay? You can work as many hours as you want each day," Maggie said.

"$1.25 an hour is very good. Thank you, Maggie. I've got a bunch of things to do at home now, but I'll be back at 3 this afternoon. Okay?" Claire asked.

"Claire, you're a lifesaver. A sweet one, and you don't even have a hole in the middle," Maggie chuckled. "Get it? A life saver but no hole in the middle?"

Claire stood up to leave and Maggie said, "Claire, don't forget your groceries by the door. I'm not going to get up to see you out. I'll be waiting for you at 3." Maggie raised her mug once again and proclaimed, "We're going to be good friends, Claire. Bye till later."

"I hope so, Maggie," Claire responded. "Thanks for the root beer. See you later." Claire let herself out and danced upstairs.

Claire was a fast yet thorough worker. Once she got familiar with Maggie's house, the dishes sparkled, the toys were back in the toy chest, and the laundry was sorted into hot and cold piles, all in less than an hour. Occasionally Maggie asked Claire to run errands in the neighborhood for her.

She got along well with Conor and Erin. She cajoled Conor if he got too feisty and she encouraged Erin to speak up when her brother started up with her. Maggie loved to talk and Claire was a good listener. They talked a lot together.

Maggie told Claire about granddaddy Shaun, about all the rest of her family, how she met her husband and how she started to have back problems when she was a teenager.

Maggie asked Claire about growing up in Poland and coming to America. Claire opened up to Maggie about the difficulty she had in making friends in school and how she spent a lot of time by herself. Claire very much liked talking with Maggie.

Maggie couldn't sing praises often enough for how Claire was a gift making her life easier.

Several months after Claire started to work for Maggie, Conor began an after-school program in judo and Erin went to an arts and crafts program. One day a week, Maggie took all three children to the library to hear the librarian read books and tell stories. Being efficient and quick, Claire now needed only one day a week to keep Maggie's house in order.

Sleepy Louie

Claire once again looked for a job to fill up her days.

Two blocks away from Claire's building was a one-room grocery store where she shopped if she unexpectedly ran out of milk or a vegetable for a soup. Claire laughed at its name – Henwood Place Fresh Market – which sounded so impressive and grand. It was a hole in the wall compared to the A&P where she preferred to shop.

In the Henwood Place Fresh Market, bins of fruits and vegetables, the canned goods and household cleaning supplies lined the two side walls. In a corner on the back wall was a lone refrigerator for milk and cheese. Next to it were a few shelves with an odd assortment of canned goods. That was the entire Henwood Place Fresh Market. A number of bare lightbulbs hung from the ceiling along the back wall, to light up the contents of the refrigerator and the back shelves. The milk and cheese and odd assortment of canned goods were a concession within the Fresh Market. The concession owner himself managed his goods. His office was a card table up against the back wall. On it was a cash register that opened by turning a crank on its side, and a pad of paper and two sharpened pencils. The concession owner sat on a folding chair with his back to the wall waiting for customers.

Claire opened the refrigerator looking for a quart bottle of milk. Finding one with a thick layer of cream on top she walked to the card table where the concession owner was sitting. He appeared to be asleep. She placed the bottle on the card table with a thud. Hearing the thud, he woke up and looked at the bottle and then at Claire.

"Twenty-four cents," he said. "You need canned peas? I just got them in today."

"No thank you; just milk," Claire replied and handed him a half-dollar.

As he put a quarter and a penny on the card table he looked again at Claire and asked, "How old are you?"

"Sixteen and a half. Why do you want to know?" she asked.

"I need help here in the store with my concession. You look strong enough to do what I need – cleaning the refrigerator and shelves; stocking them when goods come in; sweeping the back of the store. It's every day in the afternoon. Interested?" he asked.

Claire's eyes lit up. "Maybe," Claire responded. "How many hours each day and what's my pay?"

"Two hours daily and you get $1.50 a day, paid each day. Sometimes I may want you longer if a lot of goods come in at once."

"Sure, I can help you out," Claire confidently answered. "I'm ready to start tomorrow."

Chapter 10: Returning Home

"Good. What's your name and where do you live?"

"I'm Claire Bressler and I live on Henwood Place two blocks away. What's your name?"

"Call me Louie. That's good, Claire, you live nearby. It shouldn't be hard to be on time. So, tomorrow at 4. OK, Claire?"

"I'll be here at 4, Louie." Claire declared. She was so excited to have a job she turned around and bounded down the single aisle of the Fresh Market toward the street.

Before she reached the entrance, she heard Louie call out, "Claire, you forgot your milk." Claire stopped in her tracks, came back to the table and took her milk. "Thanks, Louie. See you tomorrow." she said and left.

Claire practically ran all the way home. She was so happy to have a job. *It's not the A&P but it's a job,* she told herself. She loved the buy and sell activity of business and interacting with the customers. And she wouldn't be home alone all afternoon.

She thought about the portable record player that stacked and played 45 rpms she had seen in the music shop near the A&P. *Maybe I can save up and buy it. Then I can have my own collection of records to dance to,* she mused.

When Chana came home Claire told her about the job offer. She told Chana that she'd be earning $1.50 a day.

"Good," said Chana. "We need the money. Everything costs so much these days. $1.50 a day isn't a lot, but it's better than nothing. Ask him to give you a discount on things you buy from him."

Claire stopped thinking about having a record collection.

At 4 o'clock on the dot, Claire walked into the Fresh Market.

Two young boys were at the checkout counter at the entrance of the store, asking the clerk for three cents' worth of red licorice. A lady with a screaming baby in her arms was picking tomatoes out of a bin. The lady didn't seem to hear the baby, but Claire sure did. Another lady was at the refrigerator moving the bottles of milk, looking for the cheese. There was lots of activity and noise in the Fresh Market. Claire approached the card table to let Louie know she was there on time, but he was asleep on the folding chair.

How can Louie sleep with all this noise in the store? Claire wondered. *He must be really tired. It's a good thing I'm here to help him.*

Standing right next to him Claire called, "Louie, I'm here."

Louie woke up with a start and said without missing a beat, "Right on time. First, line up the milk bottles in the refrigerator so customers can find the cheese. Then use this step stool to reach the shelves and straighten out the cans. Put the peas in front. I just got them in yesterday and we haven't had them for a couple of weeks. You like canned peas? And Claire, here's a list of everything we have in the store and how much it costs. I know all the prices without the list, but it's here for you to check if necessary. I keep it behind the cash register."

"Canned peas are okay. I like canned corn a lot more. Where's the step stool?" Claire asked. She wanted to get to work and show Louie that she was a responsible and efficient worker.

Louie pointed to a tall storage cabinet in the other corner. "In there, with the broom, dust pan, and some rags for dusting. There's an apron in there you can wear to keep yourself clean."

The lady who was at the refrigerator came to the card table with cheese and butter. She put them down on the table and said to Louie, "Can you please get me the canned peas? I can't reach them on the shelf."

Before Louie could get up, Claire said, "I'll get them."

She quickly took out the step stool from the storage cabinet. Standing on the top rung of the step stool she asked the lady, "How many cans do you want? We just got them in yesterday. They're brand new and really delicious."

"I'll take a couple," the lady replied. Claire took three cans off the shelf and handed them to the lady.

The lady said, "No, I just want a couple, just two, not three."

Claire noted to herself, *a couple means two, not three.* She had never understood that before.

The lady paid and put her purchases in her shopping cart. As she turned to go she said to Claire, "Thank you for getting the peas for me. I was only going to buy one but you made them sound so good I decided to get two."

"At your service, ma'am. I hope you'll come again when you need something," Claire politely and professionally said to the woman.

After the woman walked out, Louie said to Claire, "You're good, Claire. That was a very nice way to treat the customer. I think you're going to work fine here. Now sweep up while it's quiet." Louie sat back in his chair and closed his eyes. It looked to Claire like he was immediately sound asleep.

Claire put on the apron that was in the cabinet and took the broom. She pushed the refrigerator as much as she could to sweep behind it and emptied the waste bins. She looked around for something more to do when another customer came to the back of the store. In her arms was a baby all dressed in pink. The lady shifted the baby to her other arm so she could open the refrigerator.

Claire said to her, "Would it help you if I hold the baby while you shop?"

"It certainly would. Then I could also pick out some fruits and vegetables from the bins in the front."

Claire took the baby and cradled her in the crook of her arm. "What's her name?" Claire asked.

"Melinda. She is seven weeks old. And I'm exhausted. She's colicky and I hardly have a quiet moment to myself to do anything," the woman said. "You holding her these few moments is a great relief. Thank you."

"I love babies," Claire gushed. "I have a niece in Virginia who I used to take care of when she was a baby. Melinda will be okay with me while you shop. Take your time. I work here for Louie and we aren't so busy now," Claire said.

Giving Claire a big smile, the lady turned to the bin of apples that was near the refrigerator and began to inspect each apple she picked before putting it in a bag. Claire looked into the baby's eyes, gently bounced her and said, "Melinda, you're cute. You have such pretty eyes." Melinda cooed.

Claire looked over at Louie and saw that he was still asleep. She thought, *Louie sleeps a lot. Every time there's a bit of quiet, he goes to sleep. I wonder if he's okay.*

Another customer came to the back, saw that Louie was asleep and asked Claire, "Do you have chickpeas in a can?"

Claire hadn't learned yet what all the canned goods were, so she said, "I'll check with the boss." She nudged the card table with her foot and Louie woke up.

Chapter 10: Returning Home

"We have chickpeas in a can, Louie? The gentleman wants to know."

"No. Just the new canned peas we got in yesterday." As soon as he stopped talking, Louie closed his eyes and went back to sleep.

Claire turned to the customer. "Sorry, only regular canned peas. They're fresh. We just got them in yesterday."

"No thanks. My wife said chickpeas," and the man walked out.

Melinda started to cry and the sound woke up Louie. When he saw Claire holding the baby, he nodded, said, "Oh, it's you Claire." And went back to sleep.

Claire said to herself, *Something's not right about Louie. He doesn't stay awake. I never saw anybody fall asleep so fast and so often.*

Melinda's mommy came back with her shopping cart filled with fruits and vegetables. She took a quart of milk, a pound of American cheese and a cube of butter out of the refrigerator and put them down on the card table. Louie woke up, looked at the three items on the table and said, "$1.39." By the time the lady opened her purse, dug to the bottom to find the right change and put the coins and dollar bill on the table, Louie was once again asleep.

Claire took the money off the table, pushed the keys on the cash register to record $1.39 and cranked it open. She put the money in and closed the cash drawer. The register made a ring and Louie woke up with a start.

Claire said to him, "The lady paid with exact change. It's all in the cash register."

"Good work, Claire. I knew I could count on you," Louie told her. He leaned back in his chair, closed his eyes, and was once again asleep.

121

When Chana came home that night, Claire told her about how Louie couldn't stay awake. Chana told her that some people have something called sleeping sickness that causes people to fall asleep even when they are in the middle of doing something.

The next day when Claire came to work, there were several unopened cartons stacked against the back wall. Louie was standing next to a carton holding a knife that was stuck in the carton. He was asleep. It was clear to Claire that Louie had started to cut open the carton but fell asleep before he could finish.

That's just like Mama said. Louie can fall asleep even in the middle of doing something. He really must have that sleeping sickness, Claire thought. She said in a loud voice, "Hi Louie. How are you today?"

Louie woke up and said, "Good, Claire. You're here. Unpack these cartons of Skippy peanut butter and stack them on the shelf. Do you like smooth or crunchy?" And he pulled the knife across the package, opening it up. "Here, take a jar of crunchy when you go home today."

"Thanks, Louie," Claire answered and took the jar from him and put it in the storage cabinet. She took out the apron and went to work unpacking the jars of Skippy.

A few customers came in and Claire greeted each one. She asked if she could be of help. After each purchase she woke up Louie to tally up the cost. If Louie was asleep she took the price list out from behind the cash register and tallied the total in her head. She took the customer's money, rang up the cash register and made change if necessary.

In a quiet moment when Louie was awake, Claire said, "Louie, can I ask you something kind of personal?"

"What is it, Claire?"

Chapter 10: Returning Home

"Do you have sleeping sickness?"

"Yeah, I do. Could you tell? I try really hard to stay awake, but I fall asleep. I can't stop myself. That's the main reason why I need your help here in the store. And I can tell already, Claire, that you will be a big help to me. You are quick to go to work and find things that need doing without me telling you. And you are helpful to the customers. It's natural for you. And I believe I can trust you with the money. I hope you'll stay working here for a long time."

Claire, unused to all the praise she had just heard, blushed and didn't quite know what to say. She just said, "Gee, thanks for the Skippy. Crunchy is my favorite."

Work /Study

Half way through Claire's second year at Taft, a letter from the school's Guidance Department addressed to Chana was in the mailbox. Claire thought, *Oh no. They finally caught on that I've been skipping classes.* She steamed open the letter and read that starting the next school year, Claire's junior year, she would have the choice of three course tracks: Academic, Commercial, and Work/Study.

There was no hesitation in Claire's mind. *I'm going to do the Academic track so I can get into college and become a surgical nurse,* she told herself.

Greatly relieved that she wasn't in trouble, she re-sealed the letter and put it on the kitchen table. That night Chana read the letter and said to Claire, "The letter says starting next year you have a choice of what course work to do. Academic prepares you for college. Commercial teaches you how to work in business, as a secretary or bookkeeper or administrator. Work/Study finds you a job you do for one week and you go to class for one week. You get paid while you work."

"I'm going to be a nurse," Claire stated emphatically. "So I need the academic program to get into a college that trains nurses."

"You'll do work/study," Chana responded. "You get paid something for your work. And we need whatever money they'll pay you."

"How will I get into college if I take work/study?" Claire asked, half-knowing what her mother's response would be.

"You don't need to go to college. I didn't go to college. You can be a seamstress like me," Chana stated.

"I don't want to be a seamstress. I want to be a nurse," Claire screamed. She ran to her room and slammed the door as forcefully as possible. She believed her entire life was on the line. How could she give up her dream of becoming a surgical nurse? Claire threw herself onto her bed and sobbed into her pillow.

Finally, after what seemed like an eternity, she looked out the window. The light had changed – was the sun coming up? Had she been crying for so many hours? She knew she couldn't go on like this. Her rational voice spoke to her: *Right now, I don't have a choice, so I have to make the best decision I can. I like working and classes haven't been worth much so far. So maybe work/study will be okay. I can save some money to use it to go to college when the time comes. And I'll be away from school and home and out in the world. I'll make it good.*

As the end of the school year approached, things brightened up a bit for Claire. She was getting along well with Maggie. She liked having the responsibility of managing Louie's business since he slept so much of the time. Chana approved of Claire working, since she was earning something to offset expenses. And with vacation ahead there would be more free time to turn up the volume and dance.

Summer passed too quickly but without any unexpected challenges.

Work/study began. The first day of class, Claire recognized that many of her classmates were kids who were the not-so-bright and trouble-making ones. *This group is not headed to college*, Claire thought. *But I can go to college if I decide to.*

Early in Claire's junior year a significant change took place in her. She focused on becoming a better student. She knew that she wanted to help other people. Doing so gave meaning to her life. She reasoned: *To be a surgical nurse I have to go to college and I'll never do that if I keep skipping class. I need good marks to get into college.*

Claire transformed herself. She attended classes regularly. She said to herself about each class, *What can I learn from here that will help me be a nurse?* She read her texts carefully, making certain she understood what they said. Her dictionary became her best friend. She completed all her class assignments and turned them in on time.

One day at the beginning of the year, the first period teacher asked, "Is there anyone who would volunteer to walk two blind students to their classes each day?"

Claire surprised herself as her hand shot up in the air. "I can do it," she volunteered. She was the only one who took up the challenge. She thought, *I can help and maybe I'll make some friends this way.*

Claire was given permission to leave her classes five minutes early and arrive five minutes late so she could meet Josephine and Ron, two 11th-graders who were both blind from birth. She escorted them to their classes and then returned to her own class.

She was surprised how well the two knew the routes to take to each class and how adept they were using their canes to detect any obstructions in their path. On the third day of walking with them, Claire said to Josephine and Ron, "You don't need me to walk with you. You can get to your classes without any difficulty on your own."

Josephine said, "You're right, Claire. But Ron and I really like walking and talking with you. You talk to us like we're not any different than you." Claire smiled. It felt good to be appreciated.

The Test

In the first week of Work/Study, students took an aptitude test to determine what type of employment best suited them. Claire enjoyed taking the test because it got her thinking about the work she wanted to do. She handed the completed test to her teacher and said, "That was fun. I want to be a nurse, the kind that works with the doctor doing operations."

"You mean a surgical nurse," the teacher responded. "Well, next time our class meets you'll have the results of this test. Let's see if it agrees with you about your career plans, Claire."

When the class met again the teacher said to Claire, "The test didn't say directly that you should be a nurse. A nurse, especially in the operating room, has to take directions from the doctor and act on them without hesitation, trusting the doctor's decisions. Your test, Claire, suggested that you are best suited to being a general, like in the army. The test says you like to give orders, not take them."

Claire laughed – "A general!" And then she thought about it. "Yeah, I don't much like anyone telling me what to do," she admitted. "But if I need to learn how to take orders to be a surgical nurse, taking orders is what I have to do; I'll do it."

Claire's work/study placement had nothing to do with nursing. She was placed in the telephone call center of B. Altman, the large department store in New York City. *It's not exactly like being a nurse,* she thought, *but I'm sure I'll learn something from it. I am helping people. And I do get paid.*

She was one of a dozen women working in a large room. Each woman sat in a cubicle wearing a headset with a microphone attached. Her job was to answer a call, listen to what the caller wanted, answer a question if she could or direct the caller to the appropriate department in the store. For the entire first week, a supervisor from B. Altman sat next to Claire to teach her how to operate the phone system and respond to customers' requests and comments.

Claire quickly learned the phone system. She had fun talking to the customers and was continually surprised by the questions and comments she fielded. Her supervisor gave her lots of encouragement, seeing how bright and personable Claire was on the phone.

At the end of Claire's trial week in the call center, her supervisor said to her, "You're a natural, Claire. I usually have to sit with a student at least two and most often three weeks before I trust they can work the phone without me. You have confidence in yourself, Claire. You are much more mature than most of the high school students I've met. And you like people, don't you? I think that's a big part of why you're learning this work so quickly."

Claire took her work seriously. She was usually the first operator to show up each day and the last to leave. Before her shift she carefully tested her equipment to make sure it functioned properly. She didn't want to miss any calls because of faulty equipment. She kept her cubicle spotless. And during breaks she was friendly with all the other operators.

As part of class time at school Claire received progress reports of her work placement experience. The reports from Claire's supervisor at B. Altman were glowing.

Claire's teacher said to her, "They think you are an exceptional employee at B. Altman. I rarely get such positive comments from work/study supervisors like I'm getting about you, Claire. Keep it up. You have a bright future ahead of you."

Claire was in her element. She loved to work. She was out in the world and not cooped up in a classroom. She was meeting new people. And she was getting recognition for being conscientious and proficient in the work she was assigned. All of this contributed to Claire's ambition to be a surgical nurse.

The only setback in Claire's plans was that after receiving her first paycheck from B. Altman, Chana said to her, "It's getting more and more expensive to pay the bills. You're working now, so you can put $35 a month toward the rent."

Claire was already giving everything she earned from Louie and most of what she earned from Maggie to Chana. She said to her mother, "I want to save the money I earn at B. Altman to pay for nursing school. It's going to cost $50 a month. I want to be a nurse more than anything, Mama!"

Chana answered her emphatically, "In my family the children went out to work and what they earned was given to the parents to use for the whole family. That's how I was raised and that's how you are being raised."

If she gave all her B. Altman earnings to Mama, Claire didn't know how she would find the $50 a month tuition that was necessary to attend nursing school. But she knew that as long as she continued living with Chana there was no point in arguing with her about money.

That test was right, Claire thought. *I don't like being told what to do.*

As the year progressed, so did Claire. By the end of her junior year Claire transformed herself from being a truant to an honor student

Max

The summer between her junior and senior year, Claire's weekdays were spent working at the Fresh Market with Louie, cleaning up for Maggie, rocking and rolling with the volume turned up.

One evening Chana said to Claire, "I got a letter today from Pepi in Israel. She writes that she has a nephew, Max, who lives in New York. Pepi told him about you and he wants to meet you. Pepi's my best friend. I think you should meet him."

Max called and arranged to meet Claire the next Sunday afternoon. Chana was home when Max called for Claire.

Before Claire even had a chance to say hello to Max, Chana said to him, "So you are Pepi's nephew. Pepi and I grew up together in Poland. She never told me she had a nephew here. I wish she would come to New York to live. Haifa is so far away."

Claire stood silently beside her mother.

"Where are you and Claire going to go today?" Chana asked Max.

"I thought we would go to the Botanic Gardens at the zoo." There was an awkward silence. And then he said, "Umm. Is that Claire standing behind you, Mrs. Bressler?"

"Oh. Yes, Claire, this is Max, Pepi's nephew," Chana said and continued, "Max, sit down and tell me about Pepi. How is she getting along? Is her husband still selling flowers? When we were still in Europe I thought that I might go to Haifa to live near Pepi and sell flowers with her husband."

"My aunt is fine, Mrs. Bressler. I hope you don't think me rude, but it's getting late and if we're going to get to the gardens, we should leave now." With that, Max stood up and said to Claire, "Are you ready?"

Claire stepped forward and answered, "Ready."

As Max and Claire walked out the door, Max turned to Chana and said, "Goodbye, Mrs. Bressler. I'll have Claire back before dark. I'll be sure to let my aunt know that you were asking about her."

Claire was very impressed by Max's gentleness, good manners and respectful way of talking to her mother.

Max's behavior continued to impress Claire. The more time Claire spent with Max, the deeper she felt about him. Max was kind, caring and thoughtful. He was fresh air. Plus, he was a talented diamond cutter and had much work. For Max, the feeling was more than mutual. Whenever he had a break from work, he wanted to be with Claire.

They dated each other exclusively for well over a year. In

the spring of Claire's senior year, Max proposed marriage. He presented her with a magnificent diamond ring that he had designed and cut himself. She accepted his proposal and the ring.

Claire thought Max was a wonderful man and would be a loving husband. But one thing about Max caused Claire concern. She worried whether she could protect Max from the fallout of her difficult relationship with her mother. Claire did not want sensitive, caring Max to be damaged in any way.

On June 22, 1957, Claire made a drastic decision. She broke off her engagement to Max and returned his ring. She felt that this was the only way that she could protect Max from being damaged.

Their parting was quick and final. In the days following their breakup Claire thought, *Max is such a wonderful man. But it wouldn't be good for him or for me.*

Graduation

Claire turned her thoughts toward graduation. Work/study would end and she'd be looking for a job. She still wanted to be a surgical nurse and would have to find a college and the tuition to make it happen. She began to imagine herself on her own, free to make her own decisions on how to live her life.

A week before graduation, the lady who first supervised Claire in the call center at B. Altman came to her and said, "Mr. Savino, the director of the payroll department here at B. Altman, is looking for someone to work for him. I've recommended you, Claire. If you're interested, I'll set up a meeting for you."

"Wow. Thank you. Yes, I'm interested. I love working here,"

Claire answered. She could barely contain herself. She wanted to dance.

The meeting with Mr. Savino went well. He said to Claire, "You come highly recommended, Claire, both by your supervisor here in the call center and from what I found out about you from your work/study teacher at Taft. If you accept the position, I'll train you to operate the payroll system for the entire organization. It is a responsible job, but it sounds like you can handle it."

Claire also learned that besides her salary and paid vacation time, she would also have buying privileges of full-time B. Altman employees in the 'employees' store.'

"I'm ready to have you start working as soon as you are, Claire. Do you want to think about it? " Mr. Savino asked.

"Yes," answered Claire. And after a moment or two, Claire said, "I thought about it. I'll take the job!"

Mr. Savino laughed. "I like your spirit, Claire. We're going to get along real well."

"My graduation is next Tuesday. I have appointments on Wednesday so I can start on Thursday," Claire said.

"Excellent. But let's start Monday of next week. I look forward to seeing you here at 8:30 Monday morning. And congratulations on your graduation."

On graduation day, Claire received another surprise. Before heading to school for the graduation ceremony there was a knock at the door. Claire opened it and saw a delivery boy holding a bouquet of flowers. He said, "Claire Bressler?"

"Yes," Claire answered. And he handed the bouquet to her.

"For you," and turned and left.

Chapter 10: Returning Home

  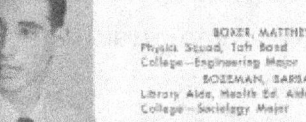  

BORRESEN, JOYCE
Traffic Aide
Business World—Secretary
BOSCARINO, SANTO
Traffic Aide
College—United States Armed Forces

BOXER, MATTHEW
Physics Squad, Taft Band
College—Engineering Major
BOZEMAN, BARBARA
Library Aide, Health Ed. Aide
College—Sociology Major

BRADY, LARRY
8th Term Rep., Traffic Squad, Track Team
Business World
BRAUNSTEIN, JACK
College—Science Major

BRECKER, DOROTHY
Taft Orchestra and Band, Attendance Office
College—Laboratory Technician
BREINDEL, GEORGE
Office Aide
College—Liberal Arts

BRENNER, BONNIE
Office Aide
College—Teaching Major
BRESSLER, CLAIRE
Yearbook Recorder
Business World
Always eager to serve her school
A good example of the golden rule

BRICKER, RAYMOND
Taft Chorus
College—Mechanics Major
BRODY, SHEILA
Teachers' Aide
College—Liberal Arts

BRODY, SIGMUND
Office Aide, G.O. Rep., Class Treas.
College—Engineering Major
BROSS, JULIUS
Taft Orchestra, Yearbook Art Staff, Traffic
Aide
College—Engineering Major

TRACK
LEFT TO RIGHT: V. Feliciano, S. Jones, V. Levy, R. Dombo, Captain; M. Schor,
T. Weinstein, H. Belsky, Manager.

CLAIRE BRESSLER IN THE 1957 YEARBOOK OF WILLIAM HOWARD TAFT HIGH SCHOOL, BRONX, NEW YORK

Claire took the bouquet and saw twelve long-stem red roses. Their fragrance filled the room. Claire read the note stapled to the wrapper. "Congratulations on your graduation, Claire. May your future be as sweet as these roses. Love, Maggie." Claire filled an empty milk bottle with water and put the roses in it. She then went down to Maggie's apartment and knocked on the door. Maggie opened the door and Claire bent down and threw her arms round the woman.

"Oh, Maggie. No one ever gave me flowers before. You are such a love. Twelve red roses. They smell so sweet. Oh Maggie, thank you," Claire said, unable to hold back her tears.

"And when the ceremony is over, you come right back here to my house. The O'Brien family is throwing you a party!" Claire peeked in and saw the house decorated with pink and white balloons and streamers hanging from the walls.

"Maggie," Claire, overcome with emotion, whispered, "no one ever made a party for me. Ever!"

"Well, you get back here; we're going to celebrate!"

Chapter 11
Bay 5 on Brighton Beach

The day after graduation, Claire and Chana moved into a summer rental in Brighton Beach. Chana needed a change of scenery and Claire was in full agreement to be by the beach.

On weekends when she could, Claire went to the beach for sun, surf, freedom and friendship.

Claire cruised back and forth between Bay 2 where the American kids hung out and Bay 5 where she met the gang from Europe, among them many landsmen from Poland. It pleased Claire that the American kids couldn't tell she was a foreigner, but she felt more at home with the European crowd.

On her second Sunday at the beach, Claire was with three other girls at Bay 5. All four were smeared with suntan lotion and lying on their stomachs facing toward the boardwalk at the entrance to the beach. A girl from Poland said to Claire in Yiddish, "Look to your left, but don't be obvious. See those two guys playing with the volleyball? They're cute. One of them comes here all the time. His name is Janyck, but he calls himself Jack. I've never seen the other one. He's new. They keep throwing the ball to each other and moving closer and closer to us."

Just then the volleyball came rolling toward Claire. She put out her arm to stop it. The ball sat on the sand next to Claire's towel. Janyck's partner came walking toward Claire to retrieve it. When he got to the ball he picked it up, smiled broadly at Claire and said, "Thanks."

"You're welcome," Claire responded, looking up at him with her sweetest smile. *He is cute,* she thought.

Janyck's partner turned and jogged back. Claire watched him as he went. She saw him hand the ball to Janyck, exchange a few words, and turn around to look in Claire's direction. Claire immediately dropped her head so he wouldn't see that she had been following him. In a couple of moments Claire saw a pair of feet next to her towel and heard Janyck's partner say to her, "OK if I sit down?"

Claire looked up and said, "OK."

As if on cue, all three girls picked up their towels and said, "We'll catch you later, Claire."

Janyck's partner sat down on the sand next to Claire as she sat up.

"So your name is Claire. I'm Kenny."

"My friend says you're new around here. Is that so?" Claire asked.

"Uh-huh. My parents live in Brooklyn but I live in Salem, in Massachusetts. Ever been there?" Kenny asked.

"No. I was in Boston when I was little, but haven't been back there since. What do you do in Salem, Kenny?" Claire inquired. It was so easy to talk with Kenny.

"I teach in a school. It's summer vacation now and I'm visiting my friend Jack. We grew up together," Kenny answered.

"You teach little kids," Claire exclaimed. And out of nowhere she said, "Tell me the story of The Three Bears."

Without skipping a beat, Kenny began, "Once upon a time there were three bears; a papa bear, a mama bear and a baby bear…."

Claire had never experienced such a spontaneous and spirited exchange with a perfect stranger before. She liked how the conversation leaped from one topic to another. Claire was fascinated and electrified to learn that Kenny's parents were Orthodox Jews and that he was a learned Jew. Claire's mind flashed back to the old men she had met in Ansbach wrapped in their *tallesim,* and felt again the magnetic draw to their swaying and singing.

When Claire heard that Kenny was a teacher in a Hebrew school she excitedly thought: *Maybe he will teach me about being Jewish.*

They made up to meet again next week right here at the beach. All the way home Claire played over her many exchanges with Kenny. Claire started to wonder if Kenny might not be the man with whom she would fulfill her sacred childhood vow.

The weeks of summer passed quickly, but they were wonderful for Claire. She and Kenny spent all their free time together, talking, laughing and learning about Judaism. As she learned more about Kenny and his Orthodox Jewish upbringing, Claire began to have thoughts about Kenny teaching her children to be *zhiden.*

The last Sunday before Kenny had to return to Salem he and Claire were at the beach with a group of their friends. In front of everyone and in a loud clear voice Kenny said to Claire, "Let's get married."

Naive and thinking to herself *Maybe one day that will really happen*, Claire said, "Sure." She was ready to accept if he really proposed.

Kenny responded, *"Harei aht mekudeshet li"*, declaring Claire his wife, uttering the phrase used in a Jewish marriage ceremony.

Claire didn't understand what Kenny's words meant, but she smiled at Kenny with her most loving smile. Several of the friends around them were Orthodox Jews and did know what Kenny's words meant. They laughed and shouted, "Mazal tov, mazal tov."

New Year's Eve

Just before Kenny returned to Salem, he and Claire told each other how much they each hoped they really would be married.

Throughout the fall, Kenny came to visit Claire as often as possible. They talked about what life would be like being married to one another, but Kenny never formally proposed.

At the Chanukah vacation break late in December, Kenny came again. By this time their discussions about married life had become pointed and personal. Claire wondered, *Will he ask me to marry him now? I'm ready. He has a fire in him that I find so exciting. And he can teach our children to be zhiden.*

Three nights before Kenny was to return to Salem he took Claire to a club in Greenwich Village to hear Shoshana Damari, known as the "Queen of Hebrew Music." As the petite Yemenite vocalist began her signature song, *Kalaniyot*, the audience applauded wildly. Kenny reached over and poured Claire a full glass of moscato wine. Claire had skipped lunch so she could go to the beauty parlor to get her hair done. She wanted to look especially good that night. She kept thinking *maybe tonight's the night he'll ask me.* And there was no time for dinner. The wine was delicious – like a spiked soda, only better.

By the time the show ended and they left the club, Claire's head was spinning. She just made it to the sidewalk before she threw up. Claire regained herself but needed Kenny to hold her arm to keep her steady as they walked to the subway. Again she threw up. And again standing on the train tracks in the subway.

Kenny said goodnight to Claire at the door of her apartment and turned to leave. Claire entered her apartment, closed the door, threw herself on her bed and began to bawl. *Oh now what? I wanted him to ask me to marry him and I'll probably never see him again. I've ruined everything.*

At 7 a.m. the next morning the phone rang. It was Kenny. Claire was pleasantly surprised.

"When will your mother be home tonight? he asked. "I want to ask her something."

"She'll be home about 8:30 tonight," she answered.

"Good," Kenny said. "We'll see you then." And he hung up. All day Claire was puzzled.

At 8:30 there was a knock at the door.

"Who could that be?" asked Chana.

"I think it's Kenny, Mama. He called this morning to ask when you'd be home. He wants to ask you something, but I don't know what it is."

Chana frowned and said angrily, "Good. I want to ask him something. Like 'what did he do to you last night that got you drunk and sick and crying like a baby?"

Claire opened the door and standing there with Kenny were his parents. Now Claire was even more puzzled. *What are they doing here?* she wondered.

"Please come in," said Claire as calmly as she could. "May I get you something to drink?"

Just then, Chana came from the kitchen. She saw Kenny and gruffly asked, "Who are these people?"

"These are my parents, Mrs. Bressler," Kenny said.

And before she could say anything more, Kenny said to Chana, "I brought my parents here tonight because I want to ask your permission to marry Claire."

Chana's anger at Kenny vanished. She looked at Kenny's parents and saw that they were smiling and nodding in approval. She looked at Claire and saw her daughter beaming.

Chana, too, smiled, and said, "Kenny, I don't know what you did to Claire last night that got her drunk and sick, but I don't care now. Yes, I give you my permission to marry Claire."

With that, Kenny and his father broke into song: *"Siman tov and mazal tov and mazal tov and siman tov."* Continuing to sing, Kenny's father whipped out a small bottle of schnapps from his pocket and put it on the table. Chana brought out little glasses and they all toasted the new couple. The two men grabbed each other's hands and danced in a circle. Kenny's mother embraced Chana and Claire.

For the first time since Chana and Claire ran from Europe there was no pain, no misery, no dark shadows of the past. At this moment, only joy and light and happiness filled the Bressler home.

CHAPTER 12

JOY AND HAPPINESS - AND THEN REALITY

Now married and living with Kenny in Massachusetts, Claire had to adjust not only to an unfamiliar environment where she knew no one but her husband, but also to a dramatic change in lifestyle.

Kenny, who was also a Holocaust survivor and came to the marriage with his own set of complications, was *shomer shabbat*, following Orthodox Jewish tradition. Their home was strictly *kosher* and they adhered to all the Orthodox religious practices. Claire was not a stranger to what needed to be done in order to have a kosher and religious home. She read a great deal to educate herself and felt she would be ready when the time came to run her own home. However, Claire had to adjust quickly to standards and explanations that were new to her.

Claire embraced this aspect of her new lifestyle. She felt secure that with Kenny she would be able to raise her children, whenever they would arrive, to be *yidden* as she promised G-d.

There were no luxuries in Claire's upbringing. She had learned how to live within the means available, no matter how meager.

Before marrying Kenny she was earning a respectable salary at Altman's and enjoyed the perk of discounted shopping at the employees' store. She liked how it felt to wear a new dress instead of the hand-me-downs she wore as a child. And being able to buy small gifts for others.

But when Claire and Kenny moved to Framingham, Massachusetts where he was teaching Hebrew, his salary, at times, didn't get them through the month. Some months there was not even enough money for food.

One morning Claire found a carton of fresh fruits and vegetables and staples on her front porch. There was nothing on the carton to identify where it came from. She couldn't imagine who would give them food but she happily accepted it. It was a life-saver.

The following week another carton showed up, again with no identifying note. Claire had to know who was doing this *chesed* for them. The next morning while it was still dark, she hid behind the curtains in the living room and peeked out, hoping to see the bearer of such kindness. On the fourth day of early-morning spying, she heard a truck pull up in front of the house. She watched a man come off the truck carrying a carton which he put on the porch. To her shock, it was the local garbage collector.

She figured out that when he came to collect the garbage, he saw that there was almost nothing in the trashcan and correctly assumed that the family had little food to eat.

It didn't take long before Kenny and Claire became the joyful parents of a baby boy. They named him Yosef after Claire's father, and called him Yossi. Claire wanted to be the kind of mother who stayed home to care for her baby like her Aunt Giza. But Claire and Kenny were in financial straits.

Claire had to find a way to supplement their income. Kenny

was home each night in the early evening, allowing Claire to take a job at Dunkin' Donuts on the late shift from 7 p.m. to 2:30 a.m. She closed the place down.

Massachusetts health laws did not allow selling yesterday's donuts, and there were always more than she could take home to Kenny. Having experienced hunger as a child, she couldn't throw away good food. She contacted a local hospital and offered them the donuts. They happily accepted, but soon had to stop because of state law. Claire then located a soup kitchen that wanted just about any usable leftovers they could find. Last thing she did at work each night was pack up the donuts and have them delivered to the kitchen.

Two more children later, Mordechai (Marc) and Dovid (David), the financial situation had not sufficiently improved. Kenny was offered a better paying position in Columbus, Ohio, so they moved. To add to their income and so she could stay at home with Dovid, her baby, Claire took in five infants, all still in diapers. The daycare work still didn't bring in enough to meet the family's needs, so Claire delivered flyers and advertisements for additional income. She went out each morning by 5:30 a.m., before her boys awakened, delivering ads in rain or shine, sleet or snow.

The boys attended Jewish day school. Claire was very pleased that they were being raised as *yidden*, but it didn't happen as she had always thought it would. From the day on the beach when she learned that Kenny was a Hebrew school teacher, she believed that he would be the one to teach her children the *aleph-beis* and so enable her to fulfill her vow to G-d. But in the end, Kenny was too busy teaching full-time during the hours that his sons were awake. When he arrived home, the boys were asleep. Ironically, Claire taught each of her boys the *aleph-beis*.

Claire was willing to do whatever work she could to ease their situation, but she and Kenny were not getting along well. The marriage was crumbling.

Claire desperately wanted to make it work, so she began marriage counseling. After three years in counseling she came to Kenny and said, "We can't continue like this. Either we go to counseling together and make corrections on the serious issues, or I'm thinking of divorce."

Kenny joined Claire in therapy for another five years, but nothing changed.

Claire did what she could to make a difficult situation bearable for herself. In the hope of making a good income to support her sons, she had enrolled in a college to earn her degree. Even though as far back as elementary school numbers and Claire were not friends, she believed that with a degree in accounting she would find a well-paying position. She applied herself and advanced through her studies. But she never had sufficient time to complete the program and get her degree. Because of her studies and her people skills, Claire worked and excelled in the accounting department of an appliance company. She went on to be Personnel Supervisor.

Two years later when both Yossi and his brother, Mordechai, were dorming in yeshiva high school and only Dovid was at home attending day school, Claire and Kenny's marriage became unbearable. Claire filed for divorce.

On Sunday, December 3rd, 1978, Claire moved out of the house. To Claire's utter shock, Dovid, age 12, had signed a paper stating that he was choosing to live with his father. At this painful and stressful juncture, Claire was completely shut out of the home and family that she had built.

Claire did find out weeks later why Dovid chose to live with his father. Understanding and deciding not to pursue to change Dovid's decision so as not to distress her son any further, she did not pursue the issue.

Claire was alone. With all her belongings packed in the car, tears welled up as she stepped off the porch for the last time. She held them back and walked to the car in the driveway. A bitter winter wind chilled her to the bone as she chipped ice off the windshield. With effort she finally got the windshield clear and entered the car. Sitting in the driver's seat, all the strength that had held her up as she walked out of her house drained from her and she sobbed uncontrollably. From her heavy sobbing and breathing the windshield iced up again. She started the motor and turned on the defroster.

She had only $50 in her purse and no prospect for more until the coming *motzei Shabbat,* seven days later. She drove down the street as if on automatic pilot, consumed in her pain. Suddenly red flashing lights appeared in her rearview mirror and a siren took her off autopilot. The red lights came right up behind her signaling for her to pull to the curb.

A burly policeman came to her car as Claire rolled down the window, with a blast of air chilling her wet eyelids.

"Your windows are iced up and your view is obstructed. Your driving is a potential hazard to others and yourself. Your license please, Ma'am," the policeman demanded.

Claire wiped the tears from her eyes and said, "I'm sorry, officer. I'll scrape the windows right now and I'll be careful driving."

"I'm sure you will, Ma'am. May I have your license please." Taking her license, he returned to his patrol car.

Claire rolled up the window and began to sob again. *How can this be happening to me?*

The policeman returned and handed Claire a ticket with a $38 fine.

"I'm sorry, Ma'am," he said. "But you were a danger to yourself and others on these icy roads. Please have control of yourself when you're driving."

Now Claire had twelve dollars left to carry her through the week. She dared not spend the money for food because she needed money for gas to get to work. *I'll eat candy bars all week*, she told herself. *I can make it. When I was with the Klimeks I survived eating rat meat after the Nazis looted our village. Candy bars are certainly better than rat meat.* Claire rationed herself to three candy bars a day.

The pain of not having Dovid to care for, not having a home of her own, failing to work things out with Kenny after trying so hard was deep. But pain was not new to Claire. From the moment her mother reclaimed her from the Klimeks, challenges and disappointments became a feature of Claire's life.

Claire felt her pain but she did not let it block her from living. She never had. Within her was the will to make life meaningful and the fortitude to keep moving forward.

The regimen of candy bars got Claire through the week. Meanwhile, friends helped Claire get resettled and she found a small two-bedroom apartment. She set aside a portion of each paycheck to purchase furnishings to make her apartment attractive and comfortable, always in the hope Dovid would soon make his home with her again.

Claire poured herself into her job and her *mitzvah* of *tahara*. For several years already she had been volunteering at the Chevra

Kadisha (Orthodox Jewish burial society) doing the *mitzvah* of *tahara*, the Jewish ritual preparation for burial. People often asked her what it was like handling a dead person.

"I'm not afraid of death," she would say. "I suppose that seeing death stare me in the face when I was six years old standing in front of a Nazi firing squad shook the fear of death right out of me. And with *tahara*, you are giving yourself totally, because the one receiving can't return anything to you. I find it the most gratifying *mitzvah*."

But she couldn't keep out her loneliness. She began to volunteer to do hospice work, spending time with people to ease their passing from the world. Comforting others was her way of comforting herself.

A Second Marriage

A year and half after her divorce, Claire met someone she hoped would relieve her of her loneliness.

Simon Greenwald (not his real name) was a survivor of fourteen concentration camps during the war. He was Jewish, but did not follow Orthodox practice. And he was sixteen years older than Claire.

Claire wanted to believe that she and Simon were meant to be married. Yet deep in her heart she knew they were not a match. Claire allowed her fear of being alone to deceive her into believing they would resolve their differences in worldview and religious practice.

Claire and Simon married. Claire made their home kosher but Simon wanted to eat out in non-kosher restaurants. Claire kept Shabbos and couldn't go in the car, but Simon wanted to travel places on his days off from work. For a year and a half they each tried to compromise, but it didn't work. Simon was a good man and he was kind to Claire, but they were not meant to live as husband and wife.

Simon finally said to Claire, "You aren't happy. Whatever I can do to help you, Claire, I will do. Take whatever you want that we have acquired. Get a divorce. And when we sell the house, take back the money that you put into it. I thought I could go back to how it was in my childhood when my family was religious, but I see that I can't."

So ended Claire's second marriage.

ADP Incorporated

Shortly after divorcing Simon, Claire found a job with ADP (Automatic Data Processing), a firm that developed automated payroll systems for businesses. When Claire started working for ADP it was a rapidly growing company, becoming a multi-billion dollar worldwide leader in automated data processing.

Claire learned the ADP systems on the job. It was the busy tax season when Claire started at ADP. She arrived each day at the office by 7 a.m. and often stayed until one in the morning. Her bosses loved her dedication, energy and willingness to learn quickly. Before ADP, Claire didn't know where the start button was on a computer.

Claire's competence and dedication became obvious to management very quickly. Within a short time Claire was asked to create a payroll program that served companies with one to 199 employees. ADP wanted to replace the outdated system they were using for companies with up to ten employees with an automated one.

Chapter 12: Joy and Happiness - and then Reality

She told her boss, "Send me to corporate headquarters in Corcoran, New Jersey where I can immerse myself in the system."

She put a sign on the door of her office saying "Maternity Leave," and went to headquarters.

After two weeks, she contacted her boss and said to him, "Give me two dozen of ADP's clients who have the most difficulty using our current payroll programs on the computer. Let's see if I can correct their mistakes. If so, I'll create the payroll program you want."

Claire interviewed the problematic clients, understanding how they were using the programs. When she understood the difficulties they were having and saw that she could solve them, she made the forms needed to report the data her system managed. She then wrote classroom instructions to teach the system and gave the classes for the new product she had created.

The product was a success. On customer satisfaction questionnaires which were sent to each client, Claire's updated program, Auto-Pay One, was successfully accepted. It was rated #1 across the entire eastern seaboard. Claire was a rising star in the young organization.

The success of Auto-Pay One couldn't be ignored. Headquarters wanted Claire to transfer to the Cleveland office to take over management of their payroll operations, because the Cleveland group was having difficulty adapting to Claire's program. She would have responsibility for the company's payroll operations at the same time she taught the Cleveland team to use her new system. Claire accepted the transfer without hesitation.

Relocating is never easy, but Claire looked forward to it. Change your place and change your luck, she told herself. She found an apartment in University Heights, and was welcomed by the *shomer Shabbos* community there.

Work went well and living in University Heights was pleasant. By now Claire was in touch frequently with her sons, though she didn't see them very often.

The Call from Rochester

One night the phone rang. It was Dovid, calling from Rochester, New York where he was learning in yeshiva.

"Mom," he asked, "may I give your phone number to someone I know here in Rochester?"

"What are you talking about, Dovid?" Claire said.

"I met an amazing gentleman here in Rochester who is *shomer Shabbos*," Dovid answered.

"No thank you. I'm not interested in meeting someone who's not in my community," Claire stated emphatically.

Dovid persisted. In every subsequent conversation he brought up the gentleman from Rochester.

Finally, Claire said to her son, "You know that I love you dearly, but I'm going to hang up on you because you refuse to listen to me." And she hung up.

A few hours later, the phone rang. Claire answered and a gentleman said, "Hello. My name is David Subar."

Claire politely responded, "Thank you for taking the time to find my phone number, but you and I have nothing to talk about. As soon as I retire, I'm planning to make *aliya* to Israel."

David then said, "So am I."

Claire stopped in her tracks and replied, "Oh, in that case let's talk some more."

And they did. David called every morning at seven before work and then at night before Claire went to bed. They talked through the month of October and up until a week before Thanksgiving. Claire became excited and hopeful.

Claire planned to have Yossi and his family come to her for Thanksgiving and Shabbos. When David heard from Claire about her Thanksgiving plans with Yossi, David announced, "I'm coming, too."

Claire thought to herself, *OK, let me see how he gets along with the family.* She hoped her son would like him.

On *Shabbos* afternoon when everyone else was napping, Claire said to David, "If we are going to get to know each other, David, there has to be *emes* (truth) between us. No masks."

David nodded in agreement.

Claire continued, "Let me start by saying to you, a person is as strong as the weakest link in their personality. I have to tell you, I'm a damaged lady and I have a lot of healing to do. I'm on my way, but I still have a ways to go. I need a tremendous amount of TLC (tender loving care). I never had it in my childhood and have not had enough as an adult. I need a husband who can share that TLC with me."

"No problem, no problem," David quickly answered. *Maybe too quickly,* she reacted. *Could he give me the love and attention I need? Could anyone?* Claire challenged herself.

The visit was a huge success and the intense long-distance phone conversations continued.

At the same time, Claire's best friend, Frieda in Columbus,

was terminally ill. Frieda was only 41. From Claire's hospice experience, she knew how important it was to spend as much time as possible with Frieda. But Claire was in Cleveland and couldn't sit by Frieda's side as she prepared to die. Claire's pain was great.

On top of her concern for Frieda, the company she worked for was going through many changes and she was fearful that she could lose her job at any moment.

In February, 1986, David asked Claire to marry him. She said yes.

They didn't wait long to marry. The wedding took place at Lou G. Siegal's Restaurant in the garment district in New York City. Claire's son, Mordechai, an ordained rabbi, conducted the ceremony. When David stepped on the ceremonial glass under the *chuppah*, the invited guests, waiters and kitchen staff at Siegel's all exclaimed, "*Mazel tov.*"

Once again Claire packed up her life, quit her job and moved to Rochester to start, once again, a new life.

Hospice in Rochester

Always concerned about others, Claire looked at hospice care in Rochester and discovered that there wasn't a facility for the Jewish community. She decided to establish the first Jewish facility and to engage volunteers from the Orthodox, Conservative, Reform and Reconstructionist communities.

"It will be a home for all Jews," she declared. And she started to build her vision.

Her first call was to the executive director of the number-one health provider in Rochester.

Chapter 12: Joy and Happiness - and then Reality

CLAIRE & DAVID SUBAR
AND DAVID'S FAMILY

"I intend to start a Jewish hospice home. Do you want to be a partner with me?" she asked him.

"No. We already service all cultures," he boastfully replied.

"Really? How interesting," Claire said. "Then I want to be one of your volunteers."

After only a few questions, the executive director realized he was talking to a highly experienced volunteer. "When can you start?" he asked.

"Not until you put me through your training," she told him.

Claire wanted to know to what extent his hospice service served all cultures, particularly Jews. She went through the training, which was good, but in no way covered cultural competence. At least not to Claire's standard.

After volunteering for a year, she started a Jewish division. She brought in twelve people covering the gamut of Jewish observance to work with her. She purchased magnetic *mezuzahs* to affix to the door as soon as a Jewish person came into a room in the facility. (The facility had rented a floor in a Catholic hospital, which had crosses in all the rooms.) She provided *siddurim* (prayer books) and Jewish reading material. The home care service provided hospice care not only in the home.

Claire didn't stop with establishing a *kosher* hospice. She wrote a two-volume instruction manual to train hospice workers serving people from twenty-two different cultures. The manual detailed customs and attitudes toward dying and death.

Claire's drive to give to others extended to all people.

Following the publication of the manual, people asked Claire, "What motivated you to begin doing hospice care?"

Chapter 12: Joy and Happiness - and then Reality

CULTURAL AWARENESS GUIDES BY CLAIRE

She would tell them, "I love giving. I cannot tell you what joy it gives me to give to others. And taking, well – I have a hard time with that. I've been taking care of people in one way or another since the day my mother took me from the Klimeks, when I was six. I became caretaker, confidante and companion to my mother. That's the way it's been. I don't know anything else. I'm not comfortable any other way."

Chana Meets Chaim

In 1958, after Claire married Kenny and moved to Massachusetts, Claire's mother, Chana, was alone in New York. Having not seen her childhood friend, Pepi, since before the war, Chana went to Haifa in Israel where Pepi was living with her husband. Chana stayed seven months with Pepi, but then her money ran out and she had to return to New York to find work. Though Pepi begged her to stay, Chana left her friend and Israel.

A few months later Chana received a letter from Pepi exhorting her, "Beg, borrow or steal the money to return here. I have the perfect man for you."

Chana returned to Haifa to meet Chaim Nieswiecki. Almost instantaneously, they clicked. They married in 1960, and returned to New York. Chana was a naturalized citizen, so as her husband, Chaim could enter the United States.

Chaim was originally from Poland. He lost his wife and baby daughter in the Holocaust. He managed to get to Russia during the war and became a tailor to Russian military officers.

CHANA

CHAIM NIESWIECKI

Chapter 12: Joy and Happiness - and then Reality

YOUNG CHAIM   CHAIM IN THE RUSSIAN ARMY

CHAIM AS A TAILOR FOR THE RUSSIAN ARMY

CHANA IN BROOKLYN

They were perfect for each other. Chana was the brains and Chaim was the hands and feet. Most importantly, Chaim had the perfect temperament for Chana. If Claire got into an argument with her mother when Claire came to visit, Chaim took Claire aside and said to her, "May I remind you of the reason why G-d gave us two ears. In/Out. Just ignore your mother when she gets like this. She is a nervous person. It's her personality. She can't help it."

The trauma of losing all of her family but Giza and having to live a false identity while serving the Nazi SS scarred Chana for life. Chana never freed herself from the guilt she carried. She survived by masquerading as a non-Jew. She did not succeed in killing Hitler when she believed she had the chance. And she had not been the kind of mother that Claire needed her to be.

The only time Chana seemed to be unburdened by her past was when she spent time tending the vegetables and flowers she grew in the small garden behind her house in Brooklyn. In her living room, every niche and corner housed plants which she lovingly nurtured.

Claire came to visit Chana and Chaim at least once and often twice a month. She cleared one shelf in the refrigerator and scrubbed it well. On it Claire had her take-out *kosher* food which she bought at a nearby kosher deli whenever she stayed for *Shabbos*. A bag with paper plates, plastic cutlery and a pot sat on a shelf in the kitchen. Chana respected Claire's observance and didn't touch the bag. Chaim looked forward to Claire's *Shabbos* visits. He particularly enjoyed singing *Shabbos zemiros* (songs) with her. Though raised in a religious home, Chana, like many survivors of the Holocaust, could not maintain her practice of Orthodoxy after the war. But she never lost her identification as a Jew.

Claire always marveled how at nearly the same time, both she and her mother had experiences which enabled each of them to break loose from the shackles of their torturous histories.

The First Hidden Child Conference, 1991

Ever since she left Europe as a child, Claire wore her 'hidden child' name tag on her heart. No matter what she did or thought, that label was part of Claire's identity.

Because she didn't know whether her memories were genuine, she didn't speak about them. *If I don't know if they're real, why would anyone believe me?* she wondered. Terrifying nightmares from which she found no relief plagued her for over seventy years. Being a hidden child was a burden Claire bore which she believed would be with her to her end.

"Thank G-d," she would later say, "Hashem has removed my burden."

In the spring of 1991, for the first time in her life, Claire met other hidden children.

On May 26th, 1991, Claire walked into the Marriott Hotel in midtown Manhattan to attend a conference billed as the first-ever gathering of children hidden during World War II.

She approached the registration desk of the conference and was greeted by a woman about Claire's age.

The woman smiled and said, "Hello. Are you here for the conference? My name is Sonia. I was hidden in a convent in Belgium, where I stayed for five years. What's your name?"

Stunned by the openness and directness of Sonia's greeting, Claire answered, "Klara Bressler. Claire quickly corrected herself. "My name is Claire Subar. I was Klara Bressler as a child."

Sonia nodded and asked, "Are you a hidden child, Claire?"

"Yes. My parents gave me to a Catholic Polish family when I was two years old," Claire volunteered. She was surprised how easy it was for her to tell this to Sonia.

"I am so happy to meet you, Claire," Sonia said warmly. "We could spend hours talking to each other, couldn't we? But there is so much to hear and learn in these two days. And so many others like us for you to meet. Here's your name tag, Claire. You don't have to be ashamed to wear it here. There are over 1,700 hidden children attending this conference."

Over the two days of the conference, Claire heard many speakers tell their stories, openly and honestly baring their souls. She attended workshops which sought solutions to challenges common to hidden children. She discovered that she was not alone in having had multiple marriages, fearing abandonment, being a workaholic and an approval seeker.

But the most seminal experience the conference offered to Claire was meeting others who, like herself, could not verify their past, who doubted their memories, and had a fragmented personal identity.

After two days of immersion with souls tormented like hers,

she walked out of the conference into the bustle of the city and for the first time in her adult life thought, *What I remember of my childhood could have actually happened to me, like it happened to so many people I met at the conference. I'm not crazy.*

Discovering that others shared similar life experiences and were trying to heal from the scars of those experiences empowered Claire to embrace her past and to stop shielding herself from it. This was a turning point in Claire's search for herself.

A Sefer Torah

Claire's mother masqueraded as a non-Jew all through the war in order to save her life and guard the hope of reuniting with her husband and her only child, who had been given away. Chana suffered greatly from hiding her true identity.

Not too long after Claire freed herself from the prison of her past, so did her mother, but in an entirely different way.

Claire's grandson, Shaya Winiarz, wrote a book entitled <u>Making a Difference</u> in which Shaya's father, Dovid z"tl, describes how Chana broke through the emotional barrier of her tortured past.

Dovid reports the events as he heard them directly from the *sofer* (traditional Jewish scribe) who interacted with Chana in the story.

My grandmother survived World War II. Her late husband [Yosef] Hy"d (may Hashem avenge his blood) was a partisan in the woods of Poland and did not survive the war.

My grandmother remarried years later to a man we called Zaidy Chaim. Together they lived for over fifty years in Brighton Beach in Brooklyn, N.Y.

In the early 1990s my grandmother decided to have a Sefer Torah written as a living memorial to her first husband and her entire family who perished in the war. She walked into a store on Coney Island Avenue, an elderly woman with only her eyes betraying all that she had seen in her life. Her posture erect, she approached the man behind the counter and informed him of her desire to buy a Sefer Torah. He led her to a shelf where the stuffed Torahs and pre-printed ones were kept – thinking she wanted a present for her grandchild for Simchas Torah. My grandmother looked at him incredulously and said, "You can't read from these!" Realizing his error, the clerk quickly called the sofer from the back of the store.

The sofer proceeded to show her Torah scrolls in various stages of preparation ranging from $36,000 and up. She chose a more expensive one, the dollar amount not being important because she understood that a Torah contains the instructions for living as a Jew. She wanted one so that those who died as Jews for Judaism would not have died in vain.

As my grandmother looked over the various Torah scrolls, she looked up at the sofer, the pain in her eyes perhaps a tad more pronounced, and asked him, "Will I be able to touch the Torah?"

Not understanding the depth of her innocent-sounding question, the sofer responded, "Of course."

My grandmother then proceeded to explain to the sofer how she had survived the war years. Being fair of complexion and having the ability to pass as a non-Jew, my grandmother spent the war years as a chambermaid masquerading as an Aryan woman with a cross around her neck in the belly of the beast – Nazi headquarters. She did this over the strenuous objections of her father who had told her on numerous occasions before he died that "it's better to die as a Jew than live as a goy."

My grandmother spent years with a cross around her neck, a cross that

Chapter 12: Joy and Happiness - and then Reality

represented the silent world who watched as the Nazis did what they would not sully their hands with. A cross that represented a religion that preached that the Jews were deserving of their fate for killing their lord. This was the cross that filled my grandmother with such a feeling of impure filth that it would be over fifty years before she allowed herself to touch a Sefer Torah.

But the time was not yet right. Months went by, and shortly before the Torah was completed, my holy grandmother visited the Coney Island Avenue storefront to see her Torah. As she saw the Torah lying on the table with the mantle embroidered with the names of her martyred family, she threw herself on the Torah and started to scream. In front of a store full of people, my grandmother's cries pierced the Heavens, where her father was crying, too.

"Tatte, Tatte, bitte zei mir moichel! Tatte, Tatte, bitte zei mir moichel!" Father, please forgive me! Father, please forgive me!" Over and over she screamed and cried. Over and over until there were no more tears. She felt she'd lived as a goy while her father died as a Jew.

And then, she stood up and looked around the shop. She spied a pair of silver candlesticks. She looked at the man behind the counter. She looked at the sofer and said, "You know, they stole my candlesticks. I really should replace them."

The sofer didn't understand who had stolen her candlesticks and asked her if it was someone in Brighton Beach and why doesn't she report it to the police. "They stole them," repeated my grandmother. "The Nazis stole my candlesticks and ever since then, I couldn't light."

To the silent people watching, my grandmother explained that for most of the years in America, Zaidy Chaim was the one who lit the candles on Shabbos because she felt she was "farschmutzed" – she was filthy.

Commissioning the *Sefer Torah* marked a release from the

suffocating grip that Chana's guilt had on her ever since the war.

Another Diagnosis

In the year 2000, Chana was diagnosed with lung cancer and a weak heart, and was given a prognosis of living only six more months. Though she had never been a smoker, the cancer was most likely the result of her working many years in a factory lined with asbestos.

After the diagnosis, whenever Claire came to visit she cared for her mother as though she were in a hospice. Claire bathed Chana, prepared food and fed her, and lay down next to her mother when she had difficulty falling asleep. Claire knew how to care for a person in the final stage of their life.

At one in the morning *motzei Shabbos*, after Chana had finally fallen asleep, Claire was sitting on the living room couch replaying thoughts and feelings about her mother and all that went on between them from childhood through her turbulent teen years.

Claire looked up and saw her mother standing in the hallway at the entrance to the living room.

"Mom, what are you doing up?" Claire asked.

"Can I come and sit with you, Claire?" she answered. "I want to ask you a question."

Chana sat down next to Claire and turned toward her.

"I don't understand you, Claire. I don't understand how you can be the way you are," Chana started.

"Why, Mom," Claire said puzzled. "How am I?"

"How can you treat me the way you do?" Chana said.

Claire couldn't imagine she was treating her mother in any way except with respect and care. Yet that's what she thought her mother was suggesting.

"How am I treating you, Mom?" Claire asked, now very concerned.

Chana's shoulders dropped and she looked straight into Claire's eyes. Her voice softened.

"You constantly come here. You love me. You hug me, you kiss me, you dance with me. You make me get nicely dressed. What's the matter with you? Why are you so good to me?" Chana asked.

Claire's mother had never spoken to her like this before. Chana was trying to connect with her daughter on an honest, open level.

Claire thought to herself, *Thank you G-d for opening the door for me.*

Her mother's openness and honesty told Claire that it might be safe to speak with Chana about dying.

She knew that her mother was terrified of experiencing pain and feared dying. Not physical death itself, but what G-d would do to her because of her past. These were topics Chana had never been able to talk about. Claire thought now she could.

Claire took her mother's two hands in hers and said, "Mom, you've got to understand something. I loved you all the years I lived with you and I've told you that. But you were never willing to listen. Now you're hearing me. That's the only difference. I'm not the one who has changed. You are! Because now you are willing to hear me."

Claire sensed that her mother was ready to hear and accept

anything Claire might say to her, so she continued.

"Another thing you have to understand: G-d will not punish you for all the things of the past."

Chana's shoulders rose and her eyes widened. "What do you mean?" she asked.

Claire softened her voice and said, "I forgave you a long time ago for everything that happened between us. So G-d is not allowed to punish you."

"Are you sure?" Chana said hopefully.

"Mom, have I ever lied to you?" Claire answered.

Sensitive to the fear of the hereafter that her mother was experiencing, Claire told Chana what she believed would convince her mother that everything will be peaceful.

"Tell me the three people whom you love the most on this earth," Claire said.

"Your father, Yossil, and my mother and father," Chana told her.

Gently squeezing her mother's hands, Claire assured her, "They are exactly who are going to welcome you home."

That was it. No more fear. Claire gave her mother what Chana needed to hear.

Sunday morning, Chana asked Claire, "What's going to happen to Chaim after I die?"

"Chaim belongs in a nursing home, Mom," Claire said flatly. "He has advancing dementia. You know that."

"No, no, no, Claire," Chana cried. "You've got to make it

Chapter 12: Joy and Happiness - and then Reality

CHANA IN HER LATER YEARS

possible for him to die in his own bed, the way you're making it possible for me."

Claire assured her mother, "Mom, don't worry. I'll take care of him. He won't go into a nursing home. I'll get someone to take care of him."

Claire returned to Rochester that Sunday. The following Thursday the call came. Her mother had passed away.

By 7:30 the next morning Claire was at the funeral home in Brooklyn where they were about to do the *tahara* on her mother. Claire knew it was inappropriate, but she requested to be allowed to be near her mother while the women perform the *tahara*.

"I beg you. Please let me in. I have years of experience doing *tahara* and teaching others how to do it," she pleaded.

Claire was allowed to put the bonnet on her mother's head. She tied the *shins*, the bows formed in the shape of the Hebrew letter *shin* on the apron and around the knees. When she had completed these steps of the *tahara* she was directed to leave.

As she turned away from the platform on which her mother

lay, Claire was unexpectedly overwhelmed by her feelings of loss. Only a week ago, Claire had experienced for the first time the openess and honesty and yes, even love, that she had craved from her mother since childhood.

Claire turned back to the table and thought, *I must let mother know that she is safe.* She bent down and gently kissed her mother on the forehead. She knew it was absolutely not permitted to touch a person after the *tahara* was performed, but she couldn't help herself.

In the house where she sat *shiva*, Claire lit the ritual candle that burns continuously for seven days. For the first three days the flame of the candle flickered wildly. During those three days Claire felt that her mother's *neshama*, her soul, was not at rest. On the fourth day the flame calmed down. Claire saw serenity in the candle and believed that her mother finally accepted her death and was at peace.

Claire returned to Rochester where she continued her life with David.

Chapter 13
Aliya

One day, more than twenty-one years after David's first phone call to Claire, when he told her that he intended to make *aliya* to Israel, he said to Claire, "I'm ready to go whenever you are."

Claire responded, "Finally, now I am going home."

In the DP camp in Stuttgart, Germany, eight-year-old Claire heard about David Ben-Gurion who said about the newly established State of Israel, "We have our own country." From that moment, Claire was ready to make *aliya*.

Jerusalem was Claire's first choice where to live. To be in the place where Jews have yearned to be for thousands of years. Who could live anywhere else? So Claire and David bought an apartment in the Arnona neighborhood, not far from the towering walls surrounding the Old City where the ancient Temple once stood.

Claire had heard from her mother many times how they had been denied immigration to the United States after the war because Claire did not pass the medical exam. This time, Claire was not going to be denied *aliya*. She and David visited every doctor who was caring for them at the time to learn exactly what medical issues they each had and what kind of doctors they should find in Israel.

Claire's primary-care doctor put her through a battery of tests, one of which indicated that Claire had a heart problem.

The doctor reported to Claire the results of the heart examination and said she could not give Claire clearance to travel by plane.

Hearing the doctor's report, Claire smiled at her and said, "With your signature, without your signature, I *will* go. And if you know me well enough, you know I will make it."

The doctor knew her patient. She said to Claire, "Then you have to give me your word of honor that when you step off the plane, the first thing you'll do is find a cardiologist."

Claire gave her word of honor and walked out of the office with the signed clearance she needed.

The next order of business was packing. What Claire and David believed they needed of their possessions filled eighty boxes which they shipped to Israel. With the remainder of their things Claire and David made a list which was sent to each of their children. One by one the children came to take whatever they wanted. After all the pickings, there were still bags and bags of usable things. The leftovers were taken to their synagogue's thrift shop. But Claire wasn't finished giving things away.

From the time she shopped at the employees' store at Altman's, Claire wore beautiful clothes that were in style. But she wasn't going to take all of them to Israel. She called some of her girlfriends to go through her closet and take whatever was hanging there.

When she immigrated to America and first entered public

elementary school, Claire suffered the embarrassment of looking different than all the other children. For a long time her wardrobe consisted of hand-me-downs from strangers. When she was finally able to have new clothing, she insisted that it be in style.

At the same time, Claire wasn't attached to her possessions. As she has said about herself: "I am very careful how I spend, because whatever money I earn ... I'm just the caretaker."

Coming Home

Finally in Israel, Claire was "home" and quickly began to make home the best place in the world for her to be. She found herself speaking Yiddish with people in her neighborhood and wanted to become more fluent. So she started and ran a Yiddish club in Arnona. She wanted to volunteer for hospice care, but David began needing more hands-on care so she couldn't get involved outside her home as much as she wanted.

As David's needs increased, the stress on Claire to care for him seriously aggravated her own health.

After five years living in Arnona, Claire and David were considering assisted-living facilities. Claire found eight and visited each one. But she was not ready for the institutional atmosphere she experienced in each one of them. Claire was not discouraged.

A full-page ad in the newspaper jumped out at her. An assisted-living facility in Jerusalem was offering a kosher dinner and a tour of the several apartments they had available. Claire said, "*Gottenu* (Hashem) sends out messages. Maybe this is a message for us."

When they walked into the facility Claire exclaimed, "David, this one isn't an institution. It used to be a hotel. It's beautiful." The dinner was tasty and they saw thirteen apartments. When they got home, Claire said to David, "If you're serious about moving into *diyur mugan* (i.e., sheltered housing), you have to tell me now. If you tell me 'yes,' then I have to be the very first one in the morning to call the sales manager. Because one of the apartments we saw is perfect for us."

David said "yes" and Claire called. She knew how to bargain. She told the sales manager, "We want to try out living in the facility for eight days. But the only apartment we will stay in for the eight days is the one we would remain in if we decide to move in." She and David moved into the apartment Claire thought was perfect for them.

The first four days of their trial stay, Claire cried. "I don't want to live here. I'll be the second youngest one here." Assistance for David was needed, but not for Claire. Drawing upon her managerial skills, on the fourth day she made a "T-Account" identifying the debits and credits of moving into the facility. The only debit she listed was being the second-youngest resident. The credit side list ran down the page.

Claire said to herself, "OK, stop with the blubbering and let's get our act together." What Claire found most positive on her list was the people, both the residents and the staff.

She said to David, "You don't live with the walls; you live with the people."

Connecting with people became Claire's primary activity in the facility. Within the first year there, Claire's people and managerial skills were recognized and appreciated. People told her that she should run the *vaad* (resident organization) of the facility.

"Talk to me in another year," she answered them. She was

interested, but she was also smart. She spent the year getting to know the people she would be working with. She understood that success in the workplace required knowing who the players are, the rules of their game and how they play by the rules. After you know all that, then you decide if you can play that game and how it might be possible to change the rules where necessary.

When the new fiscal year of the *vaad* began, Claire was asked if she was now ready to join the board. She said "yes" and in time became its president.

Caring for David

Besides the responsibilities of representing all the residents of the facility to the management, Claire's responsibilities caring for David increased dramatically. She did all the cooking for the two of them, scheduled his many doctor visits, accompanied him on all of them, and provided his daily care. In the last six months of David's life, he became blind. Given Claire's extensive hospice experience, she recognized the signs in David that signaled dementia. Claire urged David's family to visit him as often as they could – for their sake and his. She also did what she could to have people in their facility spend time with David.

David's sleep pattern changed. Morning and afternoon naps replaced nighttime sleep. Claire rested when David napped. A doctor prescribed antipsychotic medication to regulate the sleep pattern, but it didn't help. David would fall asleep and wake up and begin talking non-stop.

One day, however, the stress had built up to a level she had never experienced. Claire thought she was going to have a massive heart attack and stroke. When the symptoms subsided and she felt normal once again, Claire reacted to the incident as a signal that things had to change. She acknowledged her limits, yet wanted David to have all the care he needed.

Always concerned about others before herself, Claire thought, *If I go down, what is going to happen to David?* The next day she called an agency which sent somebody to assist her in caring for her husband.

A staff person at the facility with whom Claire was especially close told her about a psychiatric hospital in town which advises patients how they can sleep at night. The friend said the sleep program had success, and perhaps it could help David. Claire was certainly open to doing whatever possible to help David.

The hospital did not make appointments for this program. One had to show up on a Wednesday at noon and hope to be admitted. The next Wednesday Claire, David and his aide arrived at the front gate of the hospital shortly before noon. At the gate they were told that the taxi could not enter and that they would all have to walk to the sleep clinic.

Claire objected. "My husband is 95 years old, blind, and does not walk easily. You expect him to walk up that hill?"

The guard matter-of-factly said, "Those are the rules. He will have to walk in. It's not very far from here."

"That's inhumane," Claire protested.

David interrupted. "He said it's not far. Let's just do it."

The guard led them half-way up the hill and then returned to his station. Claire saw that David was having a difficult time and said to him, "Slowly, David. I'm going quickly ahead to get a wheelchair for you."

Claire ran to the sleep clinic office, opened the door, and called out to the receptionist, "I need a wheelchair immediately. Please get me a wheelchair."

"Sorry, ma'am. We don't have any wheelchairs here," the lady answered.

"Then give me some water. My husband desperately needs a drink," Claire said.

"Sorry, ma'am. There is no water available here," the receptionist said.

Meanwhile, David's aide, Roshan, realized that David could not continue walking, so he picked David up and carried him into the clinic office. Roshan put David down in a chair. Claire took one look at David, and exclaimed, "David just died."

Roshan started CPR on David. Five minutes went by before a doctor arrived who also did CPR. Ten minutes later ambulance medics who had been outside all this time came into the room and administered their heart pumps.

Claire knew that David was gone. She could see his body rising and falling from the heart pump, but there was no sign of life. One medic looked up from their efforts and said to Claire, "We're taking him to the emergency room at Shaarei Tzedek."

At the hospital David was rushed into a room, followed by the head nurse and several other nurses. A short while later the head nurse came out and stood silently in front of Claire.

Claire spoke first. "Madame, are you trying to tell me that my husband is dead?"

The nurse looked at Claire and said quietly, "Yes."

The first thing Claire did was call her son, Yossi.

"*Baruch dayan emes,*" she said to him. "I need you." Yossi immediately came to the hospital and took over what needed to be done.

My Son Dovid zt"l

On an exceptionally cold and wet winter day in January, one of the brightest lights in Claire's life went dark.

On January 18th 2015, the phone rang. It was Claire's granddaughter who also lived in Israel.

"Savta," she said, "I saw something weird on Facebook. It was something about giving condolences for the Facebook Rebbe. The Facebook Rebbe was killed."

DAVID WINIARZ ZT"L

The Facebook Rebbe was Claire's youngest son, Dovid. He was regarded as a popular rabbi in America who built a large following on Facebook, encouraging young Jewish men and women to connect with authentic Judaism.

"Don't be ridiculous," Claire automatically responded. "Dovid wasn't killed. Hang up now. I'm going to call Dovid and I'll call you right back and tell you what's going on."

She dialed Dovid's phone and her grandson, Shaya, answered.

"Shaya, this is Bubbie," Claire said, a bit anxiously, "May I talk to your father?"

"Uh uh," Shaya said.

"Why? Is he busy?"

"Uh uh."

Chapter 13: Aliya

"Shaya, is something going on?"

"Uh huh."

"Shaya, is your father dead? Is my son dead?"

"Uh huh."

"When is the funeral?"

"Tomorrow."

And that was how Claire learned that her youngest son, Dovid, had been killed in an auto accident earlier that morning. He was a passenger in the back seat, fast asleep, buckled up. The car he was in crashed head-on with another car. The cause of the crash: Black Ice. All the occupants of both cars stepped out with nothing but bruises. An ambulance was called. The medics could not understand how Dovid did not have a scratch on his body. Instead of taking him to a funeral home, they took him to the hospital and put his body through an MRI. They saw that he never woke up. Did not experience any pain. To Claire that meant that G-d picked up his soul and brought it to Shamayim.

Claire immediately called Yossi, Dovid's oldest brother. "Yossi, your brother, Dovid, was killed this morning. Will you come with me to the funeral?"

"Of course, Mom," Yossi answered. "Just tell me when."

Within an hour Yossi had reservations for both of them. When she and Yossi checked in at the reservation desk, the clerk said to Claire, "I'm sorry, Ma'am. You cannot get on the plane. Your passport expired two days ago."

Claire looked straight at the young woman behind the counter and said calmly but forcefully, "Madam, I am going to my youngest son's funeral. I need to be there."

The young woman responded, "I'm sorry, Ma'am, about your

son. One moment please while I speak with my supervisor."

In a matter of only a few minutes the young woman returned and said, "You may board now, Mrs. Subar."

Dovid's son, Shaya, wrote a book about his father. The following is an excerpt from **Making a Difference:**

> *It was a Sunday, the twenty-seventh of Teves 5775. Abba was on his way to a kiruv convention run by AJOP (Associated Jewish Outreach Programs). Abba loved going to their annual convention. He would get so excited about the fact that he was "going to a room filled with people who are interested in reaching out to Klal Yisrael." He would speak about his upcoming trip for weeks. Abba at the AJOP was like a kid in a candy store. That Sunday was a rainy cold day. The car Abba was in skidded on black ice and collided with another car. Abba was asleep in the back (wearing a seat belt, of course) at the time of the accident.*
>
> *Of course we all know that nobody dies by accident. No car can take a life without Hashem's permission. It is only a tool to carry out the will of the Creator. Hashem decided that Abba's time was up and he went home – at only forty-nine years old.*

After Dovid's passing, when people asked Claire how many children she has, she would answer, "I have three: Yossi, Mordechai and Dovid." If they asked where they live, she would say, "My oldest lives in Yerushalayim, my middle one lives now in Florida and my youngest one lives in *Shomayim* (in Heaven)."

Claire would explain that she viewed death as follows: "Our body is just a house. That's not who we are. We are the *neshama* (soul) that's inside. 'From dust you come and to dust you return.' This body goes back to where it came from. But the *neshama* doesn't die, ever. The *neshama* goes back to its Creator. It goes back home."

Chapter 13: Aliya

About Dovid, Claire proudly says, "He lived five lives in his forty-nine years. He helped to start the *bikur cholim* (visiting the sick) organization in his community. He and his wife started a furniture *gemach* (loaning furniture to people). He ran a food *gemach*. He reached out to thousands of Jews everywhere on his Facebook page, connecting them to Judaism. And many more projects I didn't even know about. All this while raising ten children and working full time. He was so busy, he barely had time to breathe."

As Claire lit her Shabbos candles, she replayed in her mind the conversation she would have with Dovid every Friday five minutes before candle lighting when he called.

Dovid: "Mom, I'm just calling to make sure you behave yourself."

Claire: "David, it's five minutes before Shabbos. Give me a break."

Dovid: "Mom...."

Claire: "OK, OK, I'll behave myself."

Dovid: "I love you, Mom, Good Shabbos."

Claire: "Good Shabbos, Dovid. I love you, too."

Talking about Dovid like this, Claire would add lovingly: "So when I go home (up there), what's waiting for him, what he's going to hear from me, is: 'You couldn't call on Friday?! You couldn't call?!'"

Claire remembers: "One time I asked Dovid, 'Dovid, I know the house in which you were raised. It was not an easy home to be raised in. How did you turn out the way you did?' As long as I live, I will never forget his answer.

'Mom, when I was a child, I didn't have any choices. The choices were made for me. But I haven't been a child for a long time. I get to make my own choices and I've chosen to be the kind of Jew that I feel a Jew should be. Why should I let the past dictate my present and future?'"

In other words, Claire believes, each of us, on a daily basis, is given the chance to make choices. Is the glass half-full or half-empty? Choices!

CHAPTER 14

THE TRIP TO POLAND

After the 1991 Conference on Hidden Children, Claire stopped distrusting the memories of her past. She wanted to discover the history which she never knew. She asked Yossi, who was named for her father Yosef, to study more about their family tree.

Yossi is a brilliant, licensed, first-class tour guide who can walk the entire length and breadth of Israel with a Tanach in his hand and show you where our forefathers trod. He knows his history. Yet, he did not accept his mom's plea to become immersed in genealogy. Claire decided to have Yossi speak with the curator of the United States Holocaust Memorial Museum in Washington, D.C. Claire was relieved when Yossi finally agreed to learn more about her family history via the many genealogy sites. Yossi started digging into Holocaust archives, but found nothing about Yosef Bressler. He wasn't discouraged.

"How could it be that there is no reference anywhere to Yosef Bressler?" Yossi wondered. "My grandfather was a soldier in the Polish army, captured by the Germans and held in prison. The Germans kept meticulous prison records and almost all of those records are accessible online."

Yossi kept searching. He came across a website referencing Polish prisoners of war. The site listed an Avraham Yosef Bressler. What little Yossi did know about his grandfather matched the information reported about Avraham Yosef Bressler. Yossi discovered that Claire's father's first name was Avraham. Claire had never heard her mother refer to her husband as Avraham; only Yosef. Claire and Yossi learned that Avraham Yosef had been sent to a notorious labor camp in Lublin, and had died either there or in Majdanek on the outskirts of the city.

Lipowastraße labour camp

The Lipowastraße labour camp, named after the street it was located on, was established as the first camp of this kind in Lublin in December 1939, and operated until the liberation, with a stoppage in 1943. It served as a detention place mainly for Jews. The special group among them included POWs – soldiers of the Polish Army captured in September 1939. Apart from that, also a group of Poles was detained here who failed to abide by the Nazi laws requiring them to supply food – the so called quotas. Before long they were released.

Prisoners confined in the camp were employed in various workshops, including tailor, shoemaker or locksmith's. In 1940 it was taken over by the German Equipment Works (Deutsche Ausrüstungswerke – DAW) – the company belonging to the SS. Among other things it produced ammunition baskets, wooden shoes and furniture.

The living conditions in the camp were very hard and the costs of prisoners maintenance were incurred by the Jewish Council. The Jews stayed in the camp until November 3, 1943, when all inmates (about 2,000) were rushed to the concentration camp at Majdanek and executed by firing squad. The mass execution was a part of the greater shooting operation, called by the SS "Erntefest" [Harvest Festival], which constituted the last phase of the Jews' annihilation in the General Government.

Today, on the grounds of the former camp, there is a shopping centre. On the southern wall of the building, the commemorating plaques were affixed.

Chapter 14: The Trip to Poland

Now Claire was shocked to remember. For some strange reason, when her third son Dovid was born, she insisted on naming him Dovid Avraham. Why Avraham, she had no idea. But it was so important for her to name him that.

LIST OF JEWISH POWS IN LUBLIN AREA CAMPS

Abraham Josef Bressler appears on this list as well. The original list is held in the Majdanek State Museum on the grounds of the Majdanek Concentration Camp in Lublin, Poland. Of the 2,933 names on this list only several dozen are known to have survived the Second World War. A minority of the rest were murdered in the camps other than Majdanek or in the forests surrounding Lublin. The majority were transferred to Majdanek and murdered there not later than the Nazi Operation Enterfest on November 3/4, 1943

183

The Reluctant Traveller

Yossi's interest in family genealogy was piqued and in 2017, he set out to locate the grave of his paternal great-grandfather. As he made the arrangements to search in Poland, he casually mentioned to his Polish colleague, Emil, that his mother had been a hidden child with a Catholic family named Klimek in the village of Debszczyzna near Lublin.

"I know that village," Emil told Yossi. "Let me see if I can find anyone from that family who is still alive and will talk with you."

Emil was successful. "There is a cousin to Mrs. Klimek whose name is Ewa. She is about your mother's age. She told me that when she was a child she played with her cousin Karolina's daughter, Wanja," Emil reported.

Yossi immediately told his mother about Ewa. "Ewa told Emil that she played with a girl named Wanja Klimek. Have you ever heard about a girl named Wanja Klimek?"

Claire gasped. She had never before revealed her Polish name to her children. Or to anyone for that matter. "Yossi, you are talking to Wanja Klimek! Emil's Ewa may be the same Ewa I must have played with when I lived with the Klimeks." Although she had no memory of her, hearing this news, Claire pushed away all her doubts and fears and decided she would go to Poland as well. Perhaps Ewa will have more information about her life in the village.

Claire thought, *Can it be I will finally learn the truth about what actually happened in the village?"*

After consulting with her husband, she called her son. "Yossi, I am joining you going to Poland"

Claire decided to go, but with great trepidation. The nightmares

Chapter 14: The Trip to Poland

and fears of meeting the village bullies of 75 years ago screamed "Don't go," but her need to know who she truly was triumphed.

Claire, Yossi, his wife Yehudit, and his daughter Sara, set out for a two-week tour of Poland. Yossi was on a mission to connect with his ancestral roots by locating his paternal great-grandfather's burial site and to learn what he could about his namesake from the Majdanek archives. Claire wanted to go to Majdanek for Yossi to recite the *kaddish* prayer for her father. No one had ever said *kaddish* for him. Claire also hoped that after meeting Ewa, she would never again doubt her past. For Claire the trip was a journey to discover herself, not a tour of Poland.

Yossi drove twenty-three kilometers from Lublin to the village of Debszczyzna (pronounced Demsh-*shiz*-na). As they entered the forest, Claire reflected on the irony of her life. "My father carried me through this forest the night he brought me to the

CLAIRE VISITNG DEBSZCZYZNA, POLAND, THE TOWN IN WHICH SHE WAS HIDDEN. WITH HER ARE YOSSI, DAUGHTER-IN-LAW YEHUDIT AND GRANDDAUGHTER SARA BAT-AMI.

185

Klimeks. And my mother walked through here the day she came to claim me after the war." Taking a deep breath, she sighed, "And now I'm coming through it with my son, his wife and my granddaughter. I never would have believed this could be. Thank you, Hashem."

Yossi drove into the village accompanied by his colleague, Emil. When they stopped in front of a small white house, Claire's heart was pounding as she sat in the backseat. She saw a short, gray-haired woman standing in the doorway of the house.

Claire opened the car door and stepped out. Ewa walked toward Claire. They met midway. Neither spoke, but stood and looked at each other for several seconds.

"Ewa?" Claire asked.

Ewa nodded and reached out her arms to hug Claire. Claire put out her arms and the former playmates embraced. Claire held back her tears.

Once inside, Ewa motioned for everyone to sit at the table where she had placed settings for each of her guests. Ewa prepared tea, fruit and homemade pastry. Emil explained to Ewa that her guests only ate kosher, but she did not understand what that meant. Claire did bring a loaf of Osem cake to share with everyone around the table. Claire was seated at the head of the table. Ewa sat to Claire's right and Emil was to Claire's left. He interpreted for them.

Claire reached into her purse and pulled out a package wrapped in plain brown paper. She handed it to Ewa and said, "This is for you."

Ewa smiled and unwrapped the package. When she saw that it was a Catholic cross she kissed it and hugged Claire.

Claire said, "It's made of olive wood from Bethlehem, Israel."

Chapter 14: The Trip to Poland

TOP: CLAIRE IN FRONT OF EWA'S HOUSE.

BOTTOM: CLAIRE AND EWA MEET

Claire and Ewa sat for several moments looking at each other. *This really is Ewa,* Claire thought. *We played together. Does she remember what happened in the village?*

Ewa broke the silence and pulled a picture out of an envelope. She showed it to Claire. A big smile softened Claire's face.

"This is me when I was sixteen," Claire said. "I included this picture to Mama in a package my mother sent to the Klimeks. Ewa, what happened to Mama and Tatu?"

"Stanislaw died in 1972, and Karolina moved to live with her sister in another town. She died in 1982."

"Ewa, do you remember what happened in the village back when we were children?" Claire asked. "There is so much I need to know."

"Please, Claire, ask me," Ewa answered.

Claire took a deep breath to quiet the pounding of her heart. She sat several moments, looking at Ewa, while sorting out the rampage of thoughts and images racing across her mind.

"Mama and Tatu had a daughter my age who looked very much like me and died a week before my father brought me to them, didn't they? This is what my mother always told me," Claire said.

"It isn't so. The Klimeks never had any children," Ewa answered.

So that is why they loved me so much, Claire thought.

"I have a memory of seeing Nazis storm into the village and kill a mother and her baby. Did it happen that the Nazis tore apart the baby?" Claire asked pointedly. She wanted to know finally if she had conjured up this nightmarish vision in her own mind, or did it really happen.

Chapter 14: The Trip to Poland

"Many years later," Ewa replied, "my parents told me that the first time the Nazis came into the village to loot it, they brutally killed a mother and child. But my parents never told me how the baby was killed. They didn't want me to know. So I don't know what you saw, Claire," Ewa responded quietly.

Then what I saw must have happened. Every parent would hide such a horrible sight from their child, Claire thought.

Then Claire asked, "Why did the two boys who beat me up every time I stepped outside always call me *jedufka*, dirty Jew? There were no Jews in the village."

"Yes, there were. The villagers were hiding a mother and her two daughters, another girl and you. Everyone knew it but did not want to draw the attention of the Nazis to the village, so no one said anything," Ewa said. "Until the mother of the boys who beat you informed the Nazis about you."

"You heard about the firing squad, Ewa?" Claire asked. Claire's pulse quickened as she sensed Ewa's answer would be a light in her search for herself. Did she dream it or did it really happen?

"I was too young and my parents never said anything to me about a firing squad, but I did hear about you standing on the windowsill and being commanded to say the church prayers that Karolina taught you."

"What happened to the other Jews who were in hiding?" Claire asked.

"The others left our village after the war. But we heard they were all killed when they tried to return to their homes."

Claire took in a deep breath. *Only I survived*, she uttered to herself, whispering a silent prayer of thanks.

"And Ewa, outside our cottage were two cherry trees that I spent hours in when Mama and Tatu were tending their field. Are they still there?" Claire asked in the softest voice.

"Everyone called them Wanja's trees. Yes, Claire, they are still there," Ewa answered warmly.

Claire and Ewa talked more about their families for a short while. Claire thanked Ewa for inviting them into her home and answering all her questions. They hugged and promised to stay in touch.

As Claire and the others were about to leave, Ewa gave Claire, Yossi, Yehudit and Sara crocheted napkins that she had made. Claire thanked Emil for helping to make the meeting and interpreting so well. Claire thanked Ewa once again, gave her a warm tight hug and said goodbye.

Claire thought to herself, *I didn't imagine my childhood. The Klimeks did love me and those terrible boys did beat me. I did climb those cherry trees and I did see what happened to the mother and her baby. Everything did happen as I remember it. All these years I've been in such doubt. Oh, to be free of that terrible burden. Thank you, Hashem, for letting me know the truth.*

"Are we ready for the next stop? It won't be easy," Yossi declared, as he pulled away from Debszczyzna and headed back the way they came.

"How could anyone be ready for Majdanek?" Claire reacted. She certainly wasn't.

"It's unbelievable," Yossi continued, "but one of the largest Nazi concentration camps was located right outside Lublin, a major city. Residents of Lublin saw the smoke rising from the crematoria and could smell the stench of burning flesh. And yet people claimed they never knew what went on at Majdanek."

Majdanek

Claire was immersed in her childhood memories. *She was peacefully in the cottage with Mama and Tatu, warming herself by the open fire. She was running outside on a bright spring day to climb Wanja's trees. She heard herself screaming as the bullies called her "jedufka" and beat her mercilessly. She felt the strength and power that emboldened her realizing she was a Jew as she faced off the firing squad.*

And then she stopped the rush of memories and thought, *It all really happened as I remembered it. Not like my mother always told me. All the pieces are fitting together. Even at this time in my life.*

She said to Yossi, "I'm ready for Majdanek."

It was early afternoon when they arrived at the visitors' entrance to Majdanek. They drove a distance and parked in front of the museum office where camp records are held and research is conducted. Only one other car was in the parking lot. They stepped out of their car into a drizzling, cold, gray sunless day.

Claire pulled her down coat around her and looked around. *My father's ashes might be right here in the ash pile in front of me. They took my father and thousands of others. But here we are. My father's grandson is coming to say kaddish for him. So many many lost. But we are still here. Thank you, Hashem, for this miracle.*

Inside the museum office they were greeted by two Christian researchers who were studying camp records of the systematic slaughter carried out by the Nazis in Majdanek.

When Yossi told them that the purpose of his visit was to learn about his grandfather, the researchers set up a microphone in order to interview Yossi and Claire about their search for

Avraham Yosef Bressler.

The researchers pulled out documents from the extensive files referencing prisoners of war who were likely exterminated at Majdanek, and laid a sheet of paper on a table.

Marta, one of the two researchers, explained in Polish that whatever information they had about Avraham Yosef Bressler was on this document.

Claire sighed deeply and thought, *All that's known about my father is on this piece of paper.*

Claire listened closely as the two researchers spoke, the woman in Polish and the man translating.

The researchers explained that Avraham Yosef Bressler was detained at the prison at Lipowastrasse 7 in Lublin, a satellite facility of Majdanek.

They went on to explain that the Nazi plan to exterminate all Jews was top secret and that records detailing the demise of Polish Jews, if they were kept, were systematically destroyed to hide the extermination plans. Reference was made to a list compiled by a reliable Jewish research institute, naming only 3,000 Jewish prisoners of war who were likely transferred to Majdanek, a number vastly fewer than the actual number presumed killed there. Avraham Yosef Bressler's name was on that list.

Claire thought, *Thank G-d, we have some evidence that my father was here in Majdanek.* Her thoughts then turned to the myriads whose end is not known for certain.

They listened as the two researchers detailed the workings of Majdanek and the Nazi system for processing prisoners.

As they thanked the researchers for their time and information and walked outside, Claire thought to herself, *My father is*

Chapter 14: The Trip to Poland

YOSSI AT MAJDANEK

YOSSI, CLAIRE AND SARA BAT-AMI AT MAJDANEK

somewhere here in Majdanek. Now he will hear his grandson say the kaddish for him. My father will know that he has a family who will never forget him or what he gave up so we could live.

The four of them walked toward the massive memorial in the center of the camp where Yossi would say *kaddish*.

When they reached the memorial no one else was there. Below them was a circular pit which held the ashes of those slaughtered and burned in the camp. They each stood in silence, enveloped in thought.

The only sound Claire heard was the wind. The massive stone monument above her was silent.

Claire turned to Yossi and asked, "How will you say *kaddish*? We need a *minyan* (ten men).

Yossi said, "You're right, Mom. And here it comes. Look!" and Yossi pointed toward the parking lot near the museum.

People were walking in the direction of the memorial.

"Savta, look," said Sara. "They're carrying Israeli flags."

When the group of about twenty-five people reached the bottom of the memorial, Claire could hear them speaking Hebrew. Yossi went down to meet them. They were employees in an Israeli aviation company. The group came to honor the memory of relatives murdered in Majdanek. When Yossi explained that he came to say *kaddish* for his grandfather, the group asked him to also have their relatives in mind when he said it.

Claire turned to Yehudit and said, "We have a *minyan!* Hashem works everything out, doesn't He?"

A *minyan* of men ascended the steps to stand with Yossi as he recited the mourner's *kaddish.*

At the conclusion of Yossi's *kaddish* the entire group responded with a resounding "*Amen.*"

Claire kept her tears to herself, but her heart was overflowing. So many years she had felt unable to connect with her father. There was nothing of her father for Claire to grasp. But at this moment Claire was with him. And she knew he was there with her.

From Majdanek, Yossi drove to Auschwitz-Birkenau. Unlike Majdanek, Auschwitz-Birkenau was a crowded site. They walked through the camps along with high school groups, organized tours and scores of individuals. Nearly two million people a year visit Auschwitz, Claire was told.

But did any of those tourists walk away angry like Claire did? As she exited through the entrance gate of Auschwitz, she looked up at the inscription above that says *Arbeit Macht Frei* (work makes free).

Claire nearly screamed. "I have enough anger boiling in me that I could kill a human monster. What have we learned from these atrocities? Have we learned to give respect to those who are different from us? Aren't racism, bigotry, and antisemitism growing with each day? Where is there peace in this world? What have we learned? And how about us, the Jews? Do we accept all Jews? Or do we also make judgments and discriminations if a Jew believes differently than our group? As my mother used to say: "Under G-d we are all His children." Does Hashem see us as labels or does He love us all?"

Father's Eyes

The last stop on their trip was in Warsaw where for the first time since beginning the trip they unpacked their suitcases. They stayed four days in Warsaw. There, Claire had an experience she did not expect.

POW CARD OF AVRAHAM YOSEF BRESSLER AT MOOSBURG

They visited the Jewish Historical Institute, a museum and research center which Yossi discovered had original documents pertaining to Jews imprisoned by the Nazis.

They inquired if the Institute had information about Claire's father. After a brief search through the files, a researcher sat Claire at a table and removed a folded paper from a plastic page protector.

THE LAST REMAINING PICTURE OF AVRAHAM YOSEF BRESSLER

He said to her, "This is the original prisoner of war record on which the Nazis recorded the detention of Avraham Yosef Bressler," and handed the folded paper to Claire. They told her of the sad fate of the forced laborers at the Lipowa Street forced labor camp in Lublin, and how the camp was shut down and the last of its inmates murdered and cremated on November 3rd, 1943. They explained where the ashes were located.

She unfolded the paper and gasped. She was looking at a photograph of her father in his Polish army uniform, and his thumbprint taken at the time of his capture. The only other picture Claire had ever seen of her father was of him in a tuxedo seated next to her mother on the joyous day of their wedding, with all their family around them.

Whenever Claire's mother described her husband Yosef, she remarked how his eyes shone with light. She could see in the wedding picture how deep and illuminating were her father's eyes. And that was how Claire had always pictured her father.

The eyes on the POW document that looked out at Claire were not shining. They were dark, dimmed, black holes.

Chapter 14: The Trip to Poland

Oh how he must have suffered, Claire thought. Her father's two sets of eyes were now burned into Claire's memory. *At least for a time his eyes shone.*

Claire put her right thumb on the thumbprint of her father and gazed into his eyes. She sat like this in silence for many minutes. And then she carefully folded the document, handed it back to the researcher and rose from her chair. It seemed to Claire that for now, all her questions had answers.

My father is more than just a story that belonged to my mother. My father now belongs to me as well.

When Claire was a youngster, she decided that her cemetery headstone in Israel was going to be an eternal monument for her father as well. His memory was going to be home, as her body would be.

In Poland, where Claire Bressler Subar lost her family, her childhood and her true identity, she found her beloved father. She took the experiences of Klartchu, Wanja Klimek and Claire Bressler and brought them into herself.

She could now return to her home in Israel. Back to the light. Back to the land of the living.

What had once been lost has now been found.

CLAIRE SEES THE LAST PICTURE EVER TAKEN OF HER FATHER

> ב׳ה
>
> Chaya (Klara) Bressler Subar
>
> A strong, spirited lady who continuously chose the path of life.
>
> וּבָחַרְתָּ בַּחַיִּים

May this stone also be an eternal monument to my father

Avraham Yosef Bressler

He saved my life during the Shoah by giving me to a loving, gentile couple who risked their lives to protect me for the duration of the war.

He was a partisaner who fought to defend humanity during the dark years. They turned his body to ashes, but his neshama, values, and family live on.

(in Hebrew Letters)	(in Hebrew Letters)
Chaya bas Avraham Yosef and Chana	Avraham Yosef ben Hersh Meier and Itte Chanzie
10 Nissan 5769 - D.O.B.	19 Teves 5671 - D.O.B. – 5 Marcheshvan 5704 - D.O.D.
April 18, 1939	January 19, 1911 – November 3, 1943

CHAYA SUBAR'S PROPOSED HEADSTONE

Family Pictures

My three sons (from l. to r.):
Mordechai, Yosef & Dovid

Lost and Found

YOSSI'S OLDEST SON & FAMILY

YOSSI'S OLDEST DAUGHTER & FAMILY

Family Pictures

Yossi's second daughter & family

Yossi's third child

Yossi's third son

Yossi's third daughter
& her dog Pele

Yossi's youngest daughter

Lost and Found

Mordechai's oldest son and family

Mordechai's second son

Mordechai's daughter & family

Mordechai's youngest son

My son Dovid & his wife Miriam
at the dedication of the Sefer Torah that I wrote

Dovid's oldest son & family

Dovid's second son

Dovid's oldest daughter & family

DOVID'S SECOND DAUGHTER & FAMILY

DOVID'S THIRD DAUGHTER & FAMILY

Lost and Found

Ozur Family
Dovid's daughter

Dovid's fourth daughter
& family

Dovid's sixth and seventh
daughters

Dovid's youngest son

www.ingramcontent.com/pod-product-compliance
Lightning Source LLC
Chambersburg PA
CBHW060951230426
43665CB00015B/2152